Right Foot Forward

Right Foot Forward

THE HOW-TO GUIDE FOR SERIOUS(LY) LIGHT HEARTED CHRISTIANS

Steve Halliday

WARNER
Faith®

NEW YORK • BOSTON • NASHVILLE

Unless otherwise indicated, all Scripture quotations are from *The Holy Bible*,
New Living Translation, copyright © 1996. Used by permission of Tyndale
House Publishers, Inc., Wheaton, Illinios 60189. All rights reserved.

Scriptures noted *Message* are taken from *The Message: The New Testament
in Contemporary English*. Copyright © 1993 by Eugene H. Peterson.

Scriptures noted NIV are taken from the HOLY BIBLE: NEW INTERNATIONAL
VERSION®. Copyright © 1973, 1978, 1984 by International Bible Society.
Used by permission of Zondervan Publishing House. All rights reserved.

Warner Faith

Time Warner Book Group

1271 Avenue of the Americas, New York, NY 10020

Visit our Web site at www.warnerfaith.com

The Warner Faith name and logo are registered trademarks
of the Time Warner Book Group.

Layout and Design: Left Coast Design, Inc., Portland, Oregon

Illustrations: Bruce DeRoos

ISBN: 0-446-69424-X

Printed in the United States of America

First Warner Books printing: November 2005

10 9 8 7 6 5 4 3 2 1

To my babe-alicious Lisa, who always helps me to know my right foot from my left. You make the journey especially sweet.

CoNTeNTS

Acknowledgments

Some books have a longer gestation period than others. This one started coming together more than a decade ago, and it never would have reached full term without the significant and deeply appreciated contributions of several dear friends and colleagues:

Bruce DeRoos — Your cartoons have made me chuckle since I first saw you put your favorite teachers in wrestling tights. Beyond that, your amazing design skills make everything work together in ways I could not envision. But perhaps most important, your good-humored partnership has made this book both possible and fun to do.

Pat Edmonds — I value our thirty-year friendship more than I can ever say. I couldn't hope to have a better collaborator for such an out-of-the-ordinary project than you and Left Coast—and I thank you for taking the risk.

Scott Ballard — More than anyone else, your unflagging encouragement, persistent urging, and downright insistence over the years that *Right Foot* get created eventually resulted in this book. I hope you're happy—it wouldn't be here without you!

Anneli Holmgren and Debbie Johansson — Thanks for your hard work and perseverance in getting everything into shape for production.

Barb Larson — Thanks for stepping in with such great help when my schedule got the better of me. Muchisimas gracias, mahalo, and gratias maximas Tibi ago!

Kathy Vick — Thanks for your support and expertise, and for getting us unstuck whenever we just couldn't get the beast up and moving.

Richard Altree, Brian DeRoos, and **Shari MacDonald Strong** — Thanks for taking time out of your busy schedules to provide some wonderful outside perspective. Each of you has influenced the final product (whether you'll admit to it or not).

The Oasis class at *Sunset Presbyterian Church* — Thanks for serving as the "guinea pigs" for much of the content of this book. I appreciate all of you!

Rolf Zettersten, Leslie Peterson, *and the rest of* **the gang** *at Warner Faith* — What a great ride it's been so far. Thanks for saying yes when it would have been much easier to say no.

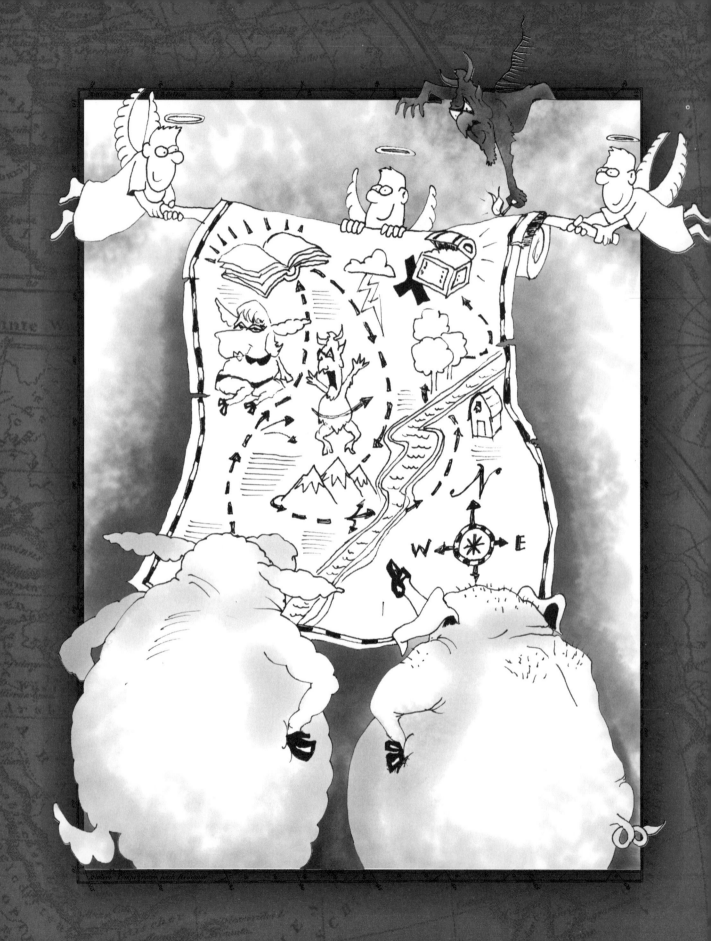

A GuiDE to INSiDE

I like to laugh.

I also like to think.

And sometimes that combination causes problems for me.

Some Christians want life to be nothing but one long laugh track. They like silly, not serious, and so if you ever try to get serious with them, their eyes start scanning for the nearest exit. I once dated a girl like that (but not much more than once).

Some other Christians look at life so gravely that they consider laughter a tool of the devil. They like serious, not silly, and so if you ever try to get silly with them, they nearly choke trying to quote you verse nine of James chapter 4: "Grieve, mourn and wail. Change your laughter to mourning and your joy to gloom" (NIV). But you know what? Despite what either of these two groups might say, I think there's room in our faith for both serious and silly, either one at a time or even side by side. Which brings us to this book. I have to tell you, it's . . . well, *different*.

I've never believed that a life of faith in Jesus Christ has to be dull, dreary, or grim. I agree wholeheartedly with the happy man who said to God, "You will show me the way of life, granting me the joy of your presence and the pleasures of living with you forever" (Psalm 16:11). I also agree with the late Elton Trueblood: "Any alleged Christianity which fails to express itself in gaiety, at some point, is clearly spurious. The Christian . . . can be sad, and often is perplexed, [but] he is never really worried. The well-known humor of the Christian is not a way of denying the tears, but rather a way of affirming something which is deeper than tears."[1]

At the same time, I also greatly admire the man who wrote, "Brothers, stop thinking like children. In regard to evil be infants, but in your thinking be adults" (1 Corinthians 14:20 NIV). And I like the words of author John Piper, who said, "There is cold knowledge, and there is a red-hot zeal that is not according to knowledge (Romans 10:2), but thinking does not have to cool your zeal. In fact, in my life, the vigorous exercise of my mind in spiritual things causes me to boil inside, not to freeze."[2]

While we want *Right Foot Forward* to be a fun experience for you, even more we want it, in at least some small way, to help you think and so grow in your faith. I know many people who struggle their whole lives to get moving in a positive spiritual direction just because somehow they never get a solid grip on the basic building blocks of a dynamic walk with Christ. We created this book largely for them. We want to start at the beginning and, as best we

can, try to describe how the Christian faith is supposed to "work," not just in theory, but in the practical, everyday events of our lives.

But as I said, it's different.

Despite all the jokes and funny quotations, it's not a joke book. Despite all the lighthearted illustrations, it's not a cartoon book. Despite the more serious main text, it's not a textbook. So what is it?

It's what I call a "kids' book for adults." I've never understood why children should have all the fun. This book's straightforward storyline and fun illustrations and sometimes goofy sidebars are all meant to work together. (And so is the "What Does *That* Mean?" section at the end. If you want to know what a **highlighted** word in the book means, just look there.) While not

everything in it is serious, nor is everything in it entertaining, we hope you find the whole package seriously entertaining (or entertainingly serious; take your pick). We know, of course, that not everyone will. More than once we've been told, very gravely, "I don't think the style of writing and the illustrations match." Well, they're right; they don't. But we never wanted them to. We see this book something like how we see life in Christ itself: serious moments mixed thoroughly and often surprisingly with lighter moments, the whole thing working as a unit to move us closer to Jesus.

For us, moving closer to Jesus is the bottom line. And on *that* point, we really don't want anything different.

Steve Halliday

---

[1] Elton Trueblood, *The Humor of Christ* (San Francisco, CA: Harper San Francisco, 1975).
[2] John Piper, *A Godward Life* (Sisters, OR: Multnomah Books, 1997), 122.

CHAPTER ONE

DeSTiNeD for GReATNeSS

All of us want to get the most out of life. We want to experience the best life has to offer—and that should go for our *faith*, too.

Did you know *God* wants the same thing? He wants us to enjoy the best He has to offer. Jesus told His first followers, "My purpose is to give life in all its fullness" (John 10:10). What a promise: *life in all its fullness!* Have you come close to enjoying "life in all its fullness"? Would you like to?

Who wouldn't?

To give ourselves the best chance of experiencing life in all its fullness, however, we have to prepare for it. And the best way to do that is to get a firm grip on how a life with *Jesus Christ* is supposed to work.

❝❝He SAiD It❞❞

You only live once, but if you work it right, once is enough.

JOE LEWIS

Some of us struggle for years in our spiritual life for one simple reason: we never fully understand who God made us to be. That's why we find it so hard to come up with good answers to three crucial questions:

Who am I?
Why am I here?
What does God have in mind for me?

Without solid, practical answers to these vital questions, some of us shuffle through life without any firm direction, fearful that nothing we do truly matters and unsure that our existence has any real meaning at all.

What a difference it makes when we hear clearly from God Himself, explaining to us who we are, why He put us here, and what He has in mind for us!

BREASTPLATE OF RIGHTEOUSNESS

BELT OF TRUTH

SWORD OF THE SPIRIT

CROWN OF RIGHTEOUSNESS

HELMET OF SALVATION

SHOES OF GOOD NEWS

Right at the very beginning of His book, the *Bible*, God tells us an astonishing fact about our true identity. Unlike any of the other creatures He made, He created human beings in His own image (see Genesis 1:27). He created *all* men and women, boys and girls—regardless of race, nationality, color, family background, height, weight, language, personal abilities, social standing, or anything else—to resemble Himself in some very important ways. None of us *are* God, of course, but as people made in His image, we reflect who He is on many amazing levels.

saying, "When God created people, he made them in the likeness of God" (Genesis 5:1). Why is murder such a terrible crime? Because "to kill a person is to kill a living being made in God's image" (Genesis 9:6). And even to curse others is a serious mistake, because they "have been made in the *image of God*" (James 3:9).

❝He SAiD It❞

You are not an accident. Even before the universe was created, God had you in mind, and he planned you for his purposes. These purposes will extend far beyond the few years you will spend on earth. You were made to last forever!

RICK WARREN

This fact is so important that the Bible repeatedly reminds us that every one of us is made in God's image. For example, when the Bible describes the first human "family tree," it begins by

MiND BeNDeRS:

Why is "if" the middle word in life?

Have you ever imagined a world with no hypothetical questions?

If you were put on this planet to accomplish certain things, and you procrastinated, would you live longer?

If you're not living on the edge, are you taking up too much space?

Why is the meaning of life so hard to find when you have a dictionary?

So what does the Bible mean when it says you are made in the image of God? Whatever it is, it distinguishes you from dogs and cats and monkeys and snakes and all other animals.

Most important, it means you have the privilege of modeling for others what God is like. When people look at you, God wants them to get some idea of His character, His goodness, and His love. He made you to be a walking advertisement for Himself!

◖◖He SAiD It◗◗

When Jesus left the earth, he commissioned his disciples to "make visible the invisible God" in the same way Christ did. The twelve healed, cast out demons, and preached "in his name" as his representatives. They were to do as he did, speak as he spoke, love as he loved, live as he lived. In a very real sense, they became his legs and arms and heart.

JOE ALDRICH

Think about that! You, like God, are in essence a *spiritual* being. That means you have the power to relate to and interact with God on a deeply personal level. God never calls the animals His sons and daughters, but He often uses such family-oriented terms to describe us. And because both we and God are spiritual beings, the Bible can say things like, "His Holy Spirit speaks to us deep in our hearts and tells us that we are God's children" (Romans 8:16). And that isn't all!

You could never be a walking billboard for God, however, if God hadn't equipped you with one very special trait: your *spirit*. The Bible does *not* say you are made in the image of God because you physically look like God. That would be impossible, for God does not have and never has had a physical body. In fact, the Bible makes it clear that God is a *spirit* (see Genesis 1:2; John 4:24). Therefore, when God created the first human, *Adam*, He created him uniquely as a *spiritual* being. Certainly, Adam had a physical body; but more important, God created him with a spirit. Why? So he could connect with God on an intimate level, something out of reach for the other creatures God had made.

While God calls His followers to be walking billboards for Him, apparently He also uses the regular kind. Consider a few that have popped up around the country, bearing His name:

➤ "Don't make me come down there."
➤ "Will the road you're on get you to my place?"
➤ "Loved the wedding, invite me to the marriage."
➤ "You think it's hot here?"
➤ "We need to talk."

God made us to resemble Him in other important ways, too. In Genesis 1:26, God says the people He created "will be masters over all life—the fish in the sea, the birds in the sky, and all the livestock, wild animals, and small animals."

God wanted Adam to rule over creation in a way that reflects how He Himself rules over it: lovingly, thoughtfully, carefully, wisely. God placed Adam in a fabulous spot we know as the Garden of *Eden* and put him in charge of it, to "tend and care for it" (Genesis 2:15). In his role as master of this new world, Adam had lots of choices to make. And what Adam decided had far-reaching ramifications for the entire creation.

Eat fruit.

"He SAiD It"

Nothing is more difficult, and therefore more precious, than to be able to decide.

NAPOLEON BONAPARTE

So what does this mean for you? It means that God has given you—as someone made in His image—the power to make life-altering choices. Your decisions can either benefit or harm both you and the creation around you. The words "But I didn't have any choice!" should almost never come out of your mouth, because as a person made in God's image, you have been given the awesome power to choose.

Yee-HAW!

In the cafeteria of a Christian school a large number of students lined up for lunch. At the head of a long table sat a large bowl of apples, with a note attached from a vigilant teacher: "Take only one apple. God is watching!" At the other end of the same table sat another bowl, this one filled with chocolate chip cookies. A hand-scrawled note, obviously from a student, offered a very different set of instructions: "Take all you want. God is watching the apples."

Eat ice cream.

Do you consider yourself a creative person? If you're like most people, you probably don't—but you really should! Because you are made in God's image, God built large doses of creativity into your very genes.

Adam proved that God had made him "in His image" when he exercised his tremendous creativity. The Bible says, "the LORD God formed from the soil every kind of animal and bird. He brought them to Adam to see what he would call them, *and Adam chose a name for each one. He gave names to all* the livestock, birds, and wild animals" (Genesis 2:19, 20, emphasis added). How many kinds of animals existed at the time Adam made his appearance in the world? Who knows? But however many there were, Adam named each one—a feat of tremendous creativity!

❝He SAiD It❞

Every child is an artist. The problem is how to remain an artist once he grows up.

PABLO PICASSO

That *same* reservoir of creativity lies within you as a person made in the image of God. Too many people sell themselves short and so never reach the potential God has put into them. As a person made in God's image, you have a creative side that can astonish both you and others . . . if you let it.

As staggering as this is, however, it doesn't convey the full wonder of who you are and why you're here. In fact, God had something even more amazing in mind when He created you.

He SAiD It

We must accept that this creative pulse within us is God's creative pulse itself.

JOSEPH CHILTON PEARCE

HiGH POiNtS in HiSToRY

In the early fifth century a little monk named Telemachus left his home in the eastern part of the Roman Empire and made his way to Rome, led by an insistent inner voice. He did not know why God was calling him to the capitol, but he felt certain that he had to go there. Once in the city he followed a large crowd to the Coliseum, where the gladiatorial games were in full swing. He had never heard of such a thing—that men created in God's own image would fight to the death for nothing but entertainment—and the sight appalled him. He jumped to the arena floor and tried to get the gladiators to stop fighting, three times calling out, "In the name of Christ!" The crowd, enraged that the monk was ruining their show, stoned him to death.

But the little monk had not died in vain. A short while later, when the emperor Honorius heard about Telemachmus's ultimate sacrifice, he ended the games forever.

Did you know that God has chosen to *permanently* connect Himself and His future to you and your destiny? To "all who claim me as their God," the Lord says, "I have made them for my *glory*" (Isaiah 43:7).

God created you for His glory! He designed you to be a living advertisement of His wisdom and power and brilliance and love. If you claim the God of the Bible as your God, then you belong to Him. You are His. You are called by His name. And it's a *big* deal to belong to God and to be called by His name.

Psalm 138:2 (NIV) tells us that God has "exalted above all things" His name and His word. *Nothing* is more important to God than the glory of His name—and He has called *you* by that name! For this reason, it makes a huge difference to God what happens to you and how you represent Him on earth. His own glory is at stake in *you*.

In the Bible, glory is a big deal. But what is it, exactly?

Glory is grandeur, splendor, honor, fame. *Glory* is what you see when a brilliant sun rises over majestic mountaintops to reveal a gorgeous, green valley fed by a roaring, sparkling river, with spectacular fields of multicolored flowers crowding its wide banks. If *glory* has a favorite word, it's "Wow!" (Although at its peak, it usually inspires a stunned reverence and awed silence.)

Glory is the Bible's shorthand way of spotlighting the indescribable majesty and perfection of God. God wants the whole world to see and stand amazed at His glory (see Exodus 33:18-12; 34:3-7; 1 Chronicles 16:24-25; 29:11; Isaiah 66:18-19)—and, unlikely as it may seem, He has chosen *you* as one of the primary channels for displaying His glory to the world.

❝ He SAiD It ❞

There are two great days in a person's life—the day we are born and the day we discover why.

WILLIAM BARCLAY

SoMeONE YoU SHoULD KNoW

Although he's been gone since 1963—he died on the same day that John F. Kennedy was assassinated—C. S. Lewis still reigns as the bestselling Christian author of all time. As a brilliant Oxford University professor for thirty-two years, Lewis effectively defended and explained the central teachings of the Christian faith to both believers and unbelievers.

Perhaps his most popular books include *Mere Christianity,* a user-friendly defense of Christianity; *The Screwtape Letters,* a fanciful work in which Lewis imagines what advice a "senior demon" might give to an underling seeking to tempt a young Christian; and The Chronicles of Narnia, a seven-book fantasy series for both children and adults intended to awaken the reader's spiritual imagination.

What continues to make Lewis so popular more than forty years after his death? Scholar Lyle Dorsett explains that Lewis avoided using the "jargon of cultural Christians. Instead, he wrote with clarity, boldness, and urgency to a post-Christian world. He used the everyday language of intelligent people, and he applied his teaching and stories to practical issues. In brief, he was a master communicator. He knew his audiences, and he pointed them to the theme of themes, Christ."[1]

Okay—but how can this Bible fact be of any practical use to you in your own spiritual growth?

For one thing, because you are created for God's glory, *your* life has ultimate meaning. All of us go through dark periods when we feel inconsequential, insignificant, overlooked, ignored, rejected. Yet despite what we may feel at these discouraging or lonely times of life, God assures us that He sees our situation, that He cares deeply for us, and that He is even now taking steps to bring us into a fabulous future.

When we begin to feel worthless or that our lives don't count for much, we often start to act in ways that look exactly the opposite of who God created us to be. Especially in these times, we need to remember that because God made us for His glory, *all* of our actions and desires and hopes carry enormous significance.

He SAiD It

It is difficult to make a man miserable while he feels worthy of himself and claims kindred to the great God who made him.

ABRAHAM LINCOLN

This is why *Paul* wrote, "Whatever you eat or drink or whatever you do, you must do all for the glory of God" (1 Corinthians 10:31). Can you brush your teeth to the glory of God? Why not? A still-quoted British preacher of the nineteenth century, Charles Spurgeon, once insisted that he could smoke an occasional cigar to the glory of God. He meant that when you live *your whole life* to make a big deal of God, even little things that don't seem the least bit "religious" point to His grace, love, and grandeur.

Because you were made for God's glory, even your "insignificant" actions carry consequences far greater than you know. So don't forget! God "called you to salvation" so that "now you can share in the glory of our Lord Jesus Christ" (2 Thessalonians 2:14).

GOD SAiD It

Can a mother forget her nursing child? Can she feel no love for a child she has borne? But even if that were possible, I would not forget you! See, I have written your name on my hand.

ISAIAH 49:15-16

HiGH POINtS in HiSToRY

It consumed almost fifty years of his political career and ended up draining him of the frail health he had always suffered, but three days before he died, William Wilberforce declared, "Thank God that I have lived to witness a day in which England is willing to give twenty millions sterling for the Abolition of Slavery."

For decades Wilberforce had fought to end the slave trade throughout the British Empire. His sudden conversion to evangelical Christianity in 1785 convinced him that he had to use his great oratorical gifts to benefit those who had no voice in Parliament (after is election in 1784, a contemporary commented on his small stature but powerful speaking presence by saying, "The shrimp grew and grew and became a whale"). Often reviled by his political opponents and cursed by the large and important financial concerns that fought to keep slavery alive, Wilberforce persevered. "God has put before me two great objects," he wrote, "the Abolition of the Slave Trade and the reformation of manners [improving the nation's decaying morals]."[2]

Due in great measure to Wilberforce's efforts, Parliament outlawed the slave trade in 1807 and accomplished the much more difficult work of emancipating all British slaves on July 26, 1833. A little more than a week later, on August 6, a grateful nation buried Wilberforce in Westminster Abbey.

But there's one even greater reason why you ought to wake up happy each morning that God created you for His glory. God has an awesome future in mind for *you*.

When God thinks of the future, He thinks of you. When He plans for heaven, He plans for you. Why? Because He has decided to merge your future with His own.

Because you were created for God's glory and your destiny is permanently merged with God's, the Bible can say of you (and of all **Christian**s), "Since we are his children, we will share his treasures—for everything God gives to his Son, Christ, is ours, too" (Romans 8:17). If you have placed your faith in Jesus, you are a co-heir with Christ, whom the Bible calls "the Lord of glory" (1 Corinthians 2:8 NIV).

None of us can even begin to picture the amazing future God has in store for all those whom He created for His glory. So the Bible reminds us, "What we suffer now is nothing compared to the glory he will give us later. For all creation is waiting eagerly for that future day when God will reveal who his children really are" (Romans 8:18-19). And that's why we can say, "Our present troubles are quite small and won't last very long. Yet they produce for us an immeasurably great glory that will last forever!" (2 Corinthians 4:17).

☞ So What?

☞ *Who are you?* You are a spiritual being capable of enjoying a deep, fulfilling relationship with God.

☞ *Why are you here?* God designed you to advertise who He is to men and women who have yet to recognize and enjoy His love.

☞ *What does God have in mind for you?* He has blessed you with awesome gifts that you cannot begin to imagine.

The Lord of the universe created you for great things and He takes a special, continual, and loving interest in you—*personally*. His future is *your* future!

SHeEP TaLK

Okay, God. I believe You have a great plan for my life. I understand You want to use me to help others get a better picture of who You are. And I'm grateful You have poured so much of Yourself into me. But where do we go from here, God? What do You want me to do today? How can I be a billboard for Your glory at home, at work, with my friends? Show me, Lord, how to successfully partner with You in what You want to accomplish in my little corner of the world. Help me, God! I pray this in the name of Your Son, Jesus. Amen.

1 Lyle W. Porsett in *Great Leaders of the Christian Church*, ed. John D. Woodbridge (Chicago, IL: Moody Press, 1988), 360.
2 http://www.chi.gospelcom.net/GLIMPSEF/Glimpses/glmps005.shtml

CHAPTER TWO

WHeRe Do I FiT iN?

lone may be the most dreaded word in the universe. And yet, who in the world has not felt lonely at some time or place?

Centuries ago the Greek philosopher Aristotle said, "No one would choose a friendless existence even if promised all the other things in the world." And much more recently, author Pearl S. Buck said, "The person who tries to live alone will not succeed as a human being. His heart withers if it does not answer another heart. His mind shrinks away if he hears only the echoes of his own thoughts and finds no other inspiration."[1]

But why? Why do we have such an enormous need for heart-to-heart relationships? Why do deep, *soul*-level attachments—relationships in which we are truly known and we truly come to know others—feel so important to us?

The answer goes to the heart of the Christian faith, to the very nature of God, in whose image we are made. And it says *you are made for relationships.*

SHe SAiD It

Remember, we're all in this alone.

LILY TOMLIN

We get a big clue about why relationships are so crucial to us when we see how God first refers to Himself in the Bible, in a passage that reports the creation of humankind. "Let *us* make people in *our* image, to be like *ourselves*," God says (Genesis 1:26, emphasis added). God does not say "I" or "me" or "my," as expected. Instead, He uses "us" and "our."

Why?

Many experts believe that in this passage the Lord hints at what we call "the **Trinity**." They suggest God uses the words "we" and "us" to help picture the eternal, loving relationships He has enjoyed within the Trinity—that is, between God the Father, God the Son, and God the **Holy Spirit**.

Sometimes when the topic of the Trinity comes up, confusion follows. So before we continue to explore the reasons behind our need for relationships, we should remember that Christians believe in only one God. Followers of Christ do not believe in many gods, all competing for attention. They do not believe in an impersonal god, so that they could say, "This stone is God." Christians believe in one living God—a *holy*, wise, eternal, and loving Lord who created all things and who rules over all.

The Bible declares, "Hear, O Israel! The LORD is our God, the LORD alone" (Deuteronomy 6:4). God insists, "There is no other God but me—a just God and a Savior—no, not one!" (Isaiah 45:21). Jesus Christ calls His Father "the only true God" (John 17:3). And the apostle Paul states flatly, "There is only one God" (Romans 3:30), whom he describes as "the blessed and only almighty God, the King of kings and Lord of lords. He alone

can never die, and he lives in light so brilliant that no human can approach him. No one has ever seen him, nor ever will" (1 Timothy 6:15, 16).

Clearly, Christians believe in only one God. *And yet . . . .*

Yee-HAW!

A pastor once visited a second grade Sunday school class. "Do any of you know what the Trinity is?" he asked. One little boy, who had just lost two of his front teeth, immediately shot up his hand. "Yes, young man?" the pastor asked. The little boy spoke quickly and excitedly, but also with a pronounced lisp caused by his missing teeth: "It'th three perthons in one God." The boy's speech impediment, intensified by the speed of his reply, confused the pastor and so he answered, "I don't understand." "That'th ok," the little boy said, "you're not thupothed to; it'th a mythtery!"

He SAiD It

The Persons of the Godhead love each other with a love so fiery, so tender, that it is all a burning flame of intense desire inexpressible.

A . W .   T O Z E R

The one God of the Bible sometimes calls Himself "we."

KiDS TaLK ABoUT LoVE

➤ Love is that first feeling you feel before all the bad stuff gets in the way.

➤ Love is when you tell someone something bad about yourself and you're scared they won't love you anymore. But then you get surprised because not only do they still love you, they love you even more.

➤ Love is what's in the room with you at Christmas if you stop opening presents and listen.

➤ There are two kinds of love: our love and God's love. But God makes both kinds of them.

This one and only God somehow exists in three "Persons."

The Bible often calls God the "Father" (Romans 1:7; James 1:27; Jude 1:1; 1 Peter 1:2, etc.). The *apostle John* writes, "See how very much our heavenly Father loves us, for he allows us to be called his children, and we really are!" (1 John 3:1).

Yet many Bible passages also speak of "the Son," Jesus Christ, as fully God (see John 5:18; 8:58; Philippians 2:6). The same Bible also clearly labels the Holy Spirit as God (see Acts 5:3-4; Hebrews 3:7-11; 9:8; 2 Corinthians 3:17).

We might feel tempted to think that the Father, the Son, and the Holy Spirit are therefore just different names for the same divine Person—yet the Bible makes it clear that the Father, Son and Holy Spirit are emphatically *not* each other (see Matthew 3:16-17; John 14:25-26; 16:12-15).

In a way we cannot fully understand, God is both one and more than one. All three Persons of the Trinity work together for a single, unified goal.

Before God created the universe and everything we see around us, He enjoyed a deep, eternal *fellowship within Himself* as Father, Son, and Holy Spirit. God never felt lonely, as some think. He has always enjoyed a perfect relationship of love within the Trinity.

And that is just the kind of love He desires for us to experience in our own relationships.

HiGH POINtS in HiSToRY

For the better part of a century, one devout and often lonely man championed the biblical view that Jesus Christ is fully God—and for his faithful work, he endured no less than five forced exiles and spent seventeen years fleeing hostile authorities.

Yet in the end, the church recognized his conviction as the gospel truth.

An Egyptian by birth but a Greek by education, Athanasius (A.D. c. 296-373) tirelessly fought the idea that Jesus was not the eternal Son of God, but a lesser being—a doctrine that attacked the truth of the Trinity, the Creation, and redemption. He responded to these errant views in a book called *On the Incarnation of the Word of God,* written while he was in his twenties. One modern scholar, G. L. Prestige, declares that Athanasius almost singlehandedly saved the church and "by his tenacity and vision in preaching one God and Savior, he had preserved . . . the unity and integrity of the Christian faith."[2]

The one God of the Bible exists in three Persons: Father, Son, and Holy Spirit.

How can three be One?!

Just as God's first reference to Himself in the Bible hints at the unique relationship between the Persons of the Trinity, so the Bible's first reference to humankind hints at our deep need for relationships. Shortly before God created the world's first man and woman, He said, "Let us make *man* in our image, in our likeness, and let *them* rule . . ." (Genesis 1:26 NIV, emphasis added). The writer then comments, "So God created man in his own image, in the image of God he created *him*; male and female he created *them*" (v. 27 NIV, emphasis added).

SHe SAiD It

The key to any good relationship, on-screen and off, is communication, respect, and I guess you have to like the way the other person smells—and he smelled real nice.

SANDRA BULLOCK

SoMeTHiNG to KeEP in MiND

No husband has ever been shot while doing the dishes.

Why talk about both "him" and "them" to describe a single humankind? It looks as if God created us to somehow reflect the relationship He enjoys between equal-but-different Persons in the Trinity. Since God refers to Himself as both "I" and "we," then couldn't it make sense that anyone created "in His image" could accurately be called both "him" and "them"?

In a way that echoes God's own nature, human beings are both one and more than one. And this fact has huge implications for our relationships.

He SAiD It

You cannot be lonely if you like the person you're alone with.

WAYNE DYER

Humans are both one and more than one—like God.

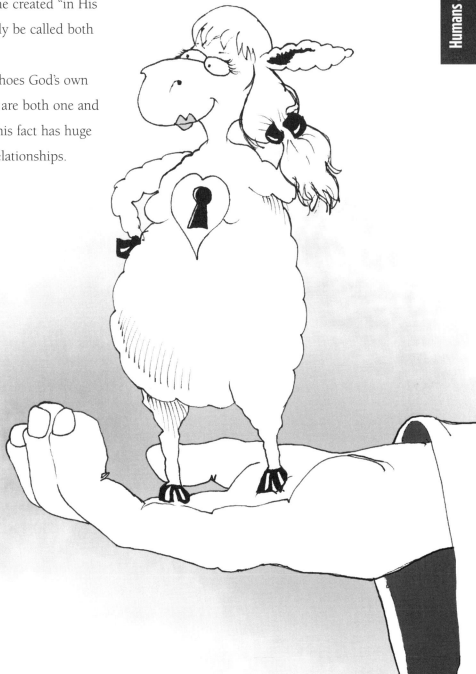

God took special care to create a beautiful place for the man He had made. Seven times God uses the word "good" to describe the world He had created. We can only imagine what it must have felt like for Adam to walk with God in the Garden of Eden without the slightest barrier in their relationship. Adam spoke directly and lovingly with His Creator. Perfect!

Or maybe not.

❝SoMeOne❝ SAiD It

When God finished the creation of Adam, He stepped back, scratched His head, and said, "I can do better than that!"

UNKNOWN

God broke the "too good to be true" mood of Paradise with the unexpected comment, "It is *not* good for the man to be alone. I will make a companion who will help him" (Genesis 2:18, emphasis added).

Wow! Remember, it is *God* who says, "It is not good for the man to be alone." Even though Adam enjoyed a perfect relationship with God, the Lord calls the situation "not good" and describes Adam as "alone."

How could this be?

IT'S ReALLY NoT GoOD

In Genesis 2:18 God declares it "not good" that Adam lived alone in the Garden of Eden. Only three other times in the Bible does God Himself call something "not good." Get an NIV Bible and look up the following three verses, and see how serious it is when God calls a thing "not good."

ISAIAH 65:2,

JEREMIAH 21:10,

EZEKIEL 20:25

When God made man in His image, He made him one and yet more than one. But before God created a second human being, the "more than one" had not yet arrived. To plug this hole, God made *Eve*, to complete the man and to allow him to enjoy delightful fellowship with someone both like him and yet different from him.

Yee-HAW!

One day, Eve went walking in the garden with God. "Lord," she said, "the garden is wonderful, and the animals and birds give me great joy, but I still feel lonely sometimes."

"I understand," God answered. "I will make a man to be your companion. He will long to please you and to be with you. But I have to warn you: he won't be perfect. He'll have a hard time understanding your feelings, he'll tend to think only of himself, and he'll stay out late with his bowling buddies."

"Bowling?" Eve asked.

"Oh . . . never mind. I was just getting ahead of Myself. Sorry."

"That's OK. I think I can handle this 'man,'" Eve replied.

"Great," God said, "I'll get busy!" The Lord started grabbing some mud and shaping it. But suddenly He stopped and turned back to Eve.

"Oh," He said, "there's one other thing about this man that I should tell you."

"What's that?" Eve asked.

"You'll have to tell him that he was here first."

SHe SAiD It

It's better for girls to be single, but not for boys. Boys need someone to clean up after them.

ANITA, AGE 9

The moment Adam saw Eve, he shouted, "At last!" And then he exclaimed, "She is part of my own flesh and bone! She will be called 'woman,' because she was taken out of a man." To cap off this story, the Bible declares, "This explains why a man leaves his father and mother and is joined to his wife, and the two are *united into one*" (Genesis 2:23, 24, emphasis added).

God intended that Adam and Eve reflect the loving nature of their Creator by enjoying a rich and deep relationship with one another. *One, and yet more than one.* Relationships are built into every cell in our bodies! That's why we hate and fear loneliness. We were made for connection.

Whom did God make for Adam? Eve, yes—but how does God describe Eve? As a spouse? No. As a mate? No. As a wife? No. He describes her as "a companion who will help" Adam.

Eve was both like and unlike Adam. Together God called them "man"; but one was male and the other, female. One had a lower voice than the other. One had a smaller physique than the other. They would spend the next many delightful days and nights discovering their surprising similarities and differences. Each considered the other a companion, an associate, a friend.

THe IDeaL MaRRiaGe

At first, Adam and Eve had an ideal marriage. He didn't have to hear about all the men she could have married, and she didn't have to hear about his mother's fabulous cooking.

God wants you to reflect His loving nature by enjoying great relationships with others.

All of us face challenges that require more than the skills and abilities that we, on our own, bring to the table. We all need assistance. We all need help. None of us can face all of life's challenges alone. God has designed human relationships to echo His own glory. We are made to build loving relationships with others who are both like us and unlike us.

You cannot find your heart's desire or fulfill your destiny without getting deeply involved in the lives of others. "A person standing alone can be attacked and defeated," says Ecclesiastes 4:12, "but two can stand back-to-back and conquer. Three are even better, for a triple-braided cord is not easily broken."

❝ SHe SAiD It ❞

Lots of people want to ride with you in the limo,
but what you want is someone who will take the
bus with you when the limo breaks down.

OPRAH WINFREY

When our relationships grow and flourish as God intended them to, we can say with the *psalmist*, "How wonderful it is, how pleasant, when brothers live together in harmony!" (Psalm 133:1).

God wants our healthy relationships to refresh the weary and satisfy the weak (see Jeremiah 31:24-25 NIV). When we treat others with respect and seek their welfare as eagerly as we seek our own—when we humbly treat others as men and women made in God's image—the world begins to see what God is really like. It almost can't help it. Jesus told us, "Your love for one another will prove to the world that you are my *disciple*s" (John 13:35).

❝❝ He SAiD It ❞❞

If a woman has to choose between catching a fly ball and saving an infant's life, she will choose to save the infant's life without even considering if there are men on base.

DAVE BARRY

A cryptograph is a puzzle in which each letter stands for another letter. The picture is a clue, either the source or the subject of the quotation.

"Ny fns'y ymj mjfy; ny'x ymj mzrnqnyd."

DTLN GJWWF

God does not call us to live as hermits, separated from the rest of humankind. If the world is to see what God is really like, it has to observe healthy, growing relationships between maturing believers who want, more than anything else, to please God and give Him glory.

This means that there are *no* mature, healthy, God-honoring, "Lone Ranger" Christians. "Just Jesus and me" will never cut it. "Give me my Bible, and God and I will be fine by ourselves" is a lie. None of us lives or dies to ourselves (see Romans 14:7). To fully reflect our Creator—and therefore to enjoy life to the fullest extent possible—we *have* to throw ourselves into significant, lasting relationships with other men and women made in the image of God.

PuZzLe TiMe!

Answer to cryptograph on previous page:

"It ain't the heat; it's the humility."

YOGI BERRA

So What?

☞ You will grow into the person God made you to be only by connecting on a deep level with others.

☞ You will make it through the challenges of a pain-filled world only with a lot of help.

☞ You most please God and reflect His loving nature when you connect deeply with other men and women made in His image.

SHe SAiD It

In Hollywood, a marriage is a success if it outlasts milk.

RITA RUDNER

Lord, you've made it pretty clear that You want me to build close ties to others, especially with those who also have committed their lives to You. Father, let me see how I'm treating others and help me to build the kind of relationships that advertise Your amazing love. Let me see *Your* model, God, and try to emulate it. Is there someone in my life whom I've been hurting? Is there someone I have been neglecting? Does someone I love need a special word or gesture from me? If so, Lord, help me to "be Jesus" to that person today. Amen.

1. http://brainyquotes.com/quotes/quotes/p/pearlsbuc121440.html

2. Samuel J. Mikolaski in *The New International Dictionary of the Christian Church*, ed. J. D. Douglas (Grand Rapids, MI: Zondervan, 1978), 81.

CHAPTER THREE

THe BiG CRaSH

It didn't take Dorothy Gale long to figure out that a roaring twister had picked her up and deposited her somewhere other than where she began. "Toto," she told her dog in the 1939 film classic, *The Wizard of Oz*, "I've a feeling we're not in Kansas anymore."

When we peek out of our own doors we don't see Munchkins or yellow brick roads, but we do see war, disease, natural disasters, violent crime, and a host of other calamities—and that makes it obvious that something has plucked us out of the perfect world God created and deposited us in a different place entirely. We all have a feeling we're not in Eden anymore.

What happened?

Genesis 3 tells us about a shattering event that radically changed the face of our planet—and the way we live on it. What happened back then continues to exert a staggering influence over the entire human race. Many Christians who fail to fully appreciate the devastating consequences of this ancient catastrophe fall into a tailspin from which they never recover. It's *that* important.

💬 He SAiD It 💬

Maybe this world is another planet's hell.

ALDOUS HUXLEY

Have you ever heard the term "The Big Bang"? It's often used to describe a gargantuan explosion thought to have given birth to the universe. Scientists tell us they can still hear "echoes" of this explosion in the form of background radiation from deep space.

The Bible describes a similarly massive explosion in the spiritual dimension that long ago devastated our world. We could call this explosion "*The Big Crash.*" Even today we can see its awful effects and hear its terrible echoes.

A T-SHiRT SAiD It

Do not disturb.
I'm disturbed enough already.

And what was The Big Crash? Although God created Eden as a paradise for the man and woman He made, these first human beings soon turned their backs on their Creator and rejected both His instructions and His loving care.

In the Bible's terms, they *sin*ned by disobeying God. God had made it clear that if Adam and Eve were to violate His explicit instructions, terrible consequences would follow. The result was The Big Crash, and it changed everything.

Before The Big Crash, Adam and Eve enjoyed a delightful partnership with each other and an exhilarating relationship with God. But all of that changed the instant they chose to depend upon themselves and reject their Creator's loving plan.

First, the sinning pair crashed emotionally. For the first time in their lives, the man and woman felt intense shame (see Genesis 3:7).

At the same time, a strange and terrifying emotional distance ripped open between them and between them and their God (see Genesis 3:8).

Immediately afterwards, they also felt something else: raw, jagged fear (see Genesis 3:10). From then on, fear would haunt them in this suddenly frightening world ruined by their own sinful choices.

But it would get worse.

MiND BeNDeRS:

Questions no Sunday School Teacher Wants to Hear

If God did't make the sun until the fourth day, then where did the light come from on the first three days?

If God is all-powerful, then why did He have to take a day off from work to rest?

If Adam and Eve could be naked and feel no shame, then why do I have to wear clothes?

After The Big Crash brought shame, alienation, fear, blame-shifting, frustration, staggering pain, and sharp conflict into a perfect world that had known none of it, it topped off its bitter sundae with the deadliest cherry of all: death.

God told the disobedient couple that they would "return to the ground from which you came. For you were made from dust, and to the dust you will return" (Genesis 3:19). How could Adam and Eve continue to live in peace when by their disobedience they had severed their link to the only Source of life and peace?

The Big Crash warped life on this planet in grotesque ways. The results of Adam and Eve's sin continue to plague us today.

God did not design this world for thorns, thistles, pain, conflict, and aggravation. He certainly did not design it as a showplace for death. And yet, The Big Crash has brought all of those things to our doorstep.

We don't live in Eden anymore, Toto.

When God banished Adam and Eve from the Garden of Eden, he banished us, too (see Genesis 3:23-24). The rule is simple: you sin, you die (see Deuteronomy 24:16; Romans 6:23). There are no exceptions. And the place for those who have sinned is not in a perfect paradise like Eden, but in a warped world like this.

Of course, it's not easy to live in a *curse*d world. It's no fun. But you know what? It's not supposed to be.

Think of it like this. Suppose you had a kind of cancer that could be cured—but only if the disease were discovered in time. Let's say that this cancer caused you terrific pain. Now, is that pain a good thing or a bad thing? It depends. If it causes you to seek treatment and find a cure, the pain actually works to your advantage. And if you ignore the pain? Then you die, and the pain really was your enemy all along.

FaMoUS LaST WoRDS

"Am I dying or is this my birthday?"
LADY ASTOR

"Friends applaud, the comedy is over."
LUDWIG VON BEETHOVEN

"So little done, so much to do."
CECIL JOHN RHODES

"Go away. I'm all right."
H. G. WELLS

"Don't let it end like this. Tell them I said something!"
PANCHO VILLA

The Big Crash brought death into our world.

❝SoMeOne❞ SAiD It

Be sure to live your life, because you are a long time dead.
SCOTTISH PROVERB

Because we're human, most of us, at least once in a while, blame God for the hurt we endure. When a tragedy occurs, we cry out, "Why, God? If You're so good and loving, why do You allow such evil? If You're all-powerful, why don't You stop it? If You're all-knowing, why don't You tell us how to avoid it?"

God understands our tendency to ask such questions, because we've been asking them for a long, long time.

The QUeSTiON BoX

1. If God promised to answer any one of your "why" questions, what would you ask Him?
2. If God were to ask you a "why" question about some choice you've made, what do you think He'd ask?

But you know something? Rarely, if ever, does He give us the answers we demand. Often He remains silent about why He allowed some evil to take place or some tragedy to occur.

He consistently reminds us, however, that we live on a diseased planet—and the disease has fully infected each one of us.

A group of people once approached Jesus to ask why God allowed a brutal Roman governor to attack and kill some pious Jews who had done nothing but travel to *Jerusalem* to worship in the *temple*. Jesus' answer made them gasp.

"Do you think those Galileans were worse sinners than other people from Galilee? Is that why they suffered?" Jesus asked. "Not at all! And you will also perish unless you turn from your evil ways and turn to God."

Insensitive? Many in the crowd probably thought so. But then Jesus brought up another tragedy no one had even inquired about.

HoLLyWoOD THeOLoGY
ON THE PROBLEM OF PAIN . . .

"Life is pain, Highness. Anyone who says differently is selling something."

WESTLEY IN
"THE PRINCESS BRIDE"

"And what about the eighteen men who died when the Tower of Siloam fell on them?" He continued. "Were they the worst sinners in Jerusalem? No, and I tell you again that unless you repent, you will also perish" (Luke 13:2-5).

💬 He SAiD It 💬

When the London *Times* asked several celebrities to suggest an answer to the question "What's wrong with the world?" a popular author wrote,

Dear Sirs:

I am.

Sincerely, G. K. Chesterton

Why would the man later known as "the Good Shepherd" say things that sound so tactless, so blunt? He spoke like this because He is also called "the Great Physician," and as a top-flight doctor fully acquainted with our spiritual condition, He wants to give us a clear diagnosis. Yes, it's painful to live in a world warped and twisted by sin; but God wants to use our pain (and the pain of others similarly infected) to alert us to our dire situation.

The prophet Amos declared that God sometimes uses hunger, scarcity, drought, crop failure, plagues, war, and natural disasters to bring spiritually

Yee-HAW!

After feeling a little under the weather for a couple of days, a man made an appointment to see his doctor. After the examination, the doctor looked at the man and said gravely, "You'd better sit down."

"What is it, Doc?" the worried man asked.

"I'm afraid I have bad news," the doctor replied. "You're dying, and you don't have much time left."

The stricken man went pale and asked weakly, "Well, how long do I have?"

"10," the doctor answered.

"10?" the confused man said. "10 what? Months? Weeks?"

"10 … 9 … 8 … 7 …"

❝ He SAiD It ❞

Pain is God's megaphone to a deaf world.

C. S. LEWIS

wandering men and women back into a close relationship with Himself (see Amos 4:6–11). The Bible insists that although God "does not enjoy hurting people or causing them sorrow" (Lamentations 3:33), yet in His love He will use even these things to bring us back to Himself. "Now return to me," God says, "and I will return to you" (Malachi 3:7).

God did not curse the earth after The Big Crash in order to destroy us but to alert us to our mortal danger and so to lead us away from eternal destruction and into everlasting life. Although it hurts to live in a cursed world, our pain reminds us that God wants something infinitely better for us.

Still, the Lord has no intention of allowing this warped world to continue on its crooked path forever. A bright, new day is coming . . . and true to form, God began planning for it even before Adam and Eve took their disastrous first steps into spiritual revolt.

SHe SAiD It

Our ancestors lived in two worlds, and understood this to be the solitary, poor, nasty, brutish and short one. We are the first generation of man that actually expected to find happiness on earth, and our search for it has caused such unhappiness . . . The reason: If you do not believe in another, higher world, if you believe only in the flat, material world around you, if you believe that this is your only chance at happiness—if that is what you believe, then you are not disappointed when the world does not give you a good measure of its riches; you are despairing.

PEGGY NOONAN

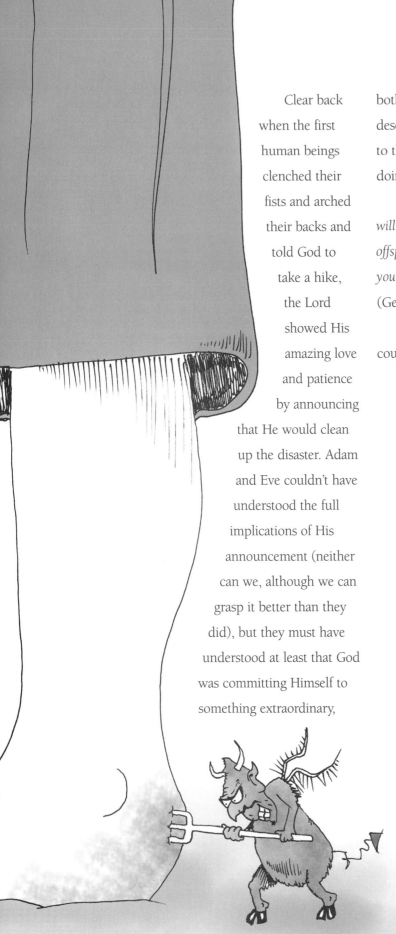

Clear back when the first human beings clenched their fists and arched their backs and told God to take a hike, the Lord showed His amazing love and patience by announcing that He would clean up the disaster. Adam and Eve couldn't have understood the full implications of His announcement (neither can we, although we can grasp it better than they did), but they must have understood at least that God was committing Himself to something extraordinary, both for their benefit and for that of their descendants. Listen to God's veiled words to the serpent who manipulated Eve into doing what God had prohibited:

From now on, you and the woman will be enemies, and your offspring and her offspring will be enemies. He will crush your head, and you will strike his heel. (Genesis 3:15)

What did it mean? Far more than we could ever have **hope**d.

❝ He SAiD It ❞

Satan put into the heads of our remote ancestors . . . the idea that they could "be like gods," could set up on their own as if they had created themselves, be their own masters, invent some sort of happiness for themselves outside God, apart from God. And out of that hopeless attempt has come nearly all that we call human history: poverty, ambition, war, prostitution, classes, empires, slavery—the long, terrible story of man trying to find something other than God which will make him happy.

C. S. LEWIS

❝ He SAiD It ❞

Jesus Christ turns life right-side up,
and heaven outside-in.

CARL F. H. HENRY

From our vantage point in time, we recognize these amazing words as the first **prophecy** in the Bible concerning the work of Jesus Christ. They provide the background for the most famous verse in Scripture: "For God so loved the world that he gave his only Son, that everyone who believes in him will not perish but have **eternal life**" (John 3:16). Jesus Christ came to earth to give us back what Adam lost (and then some!).

In fact, Adam didn't even have time to pick the **forbidden fruit** from between his teeth before God set in motion a breathtaking plan to rescue both him and his doomed offspring. No one—not Adam, his children, or us—can escape the consequences of sin. Remember the **law**? You sin, you die.

But in His amazing love, God provided a way for us to escape the penalty for our disobedience without violating His law. How? Someone else— Jesus Christ, the second Person of the Trinity —would voluntarily take our place and endure the full force of the death sentence that we earned.

The apostle Paul explains what happened like this: "If one man's sin put crowds of people at the dead-end abyss of separation from God, just think what God's gift poured through one man, Jesus Christ, will do! There's no comparison between that death-dealing sin and this generous, life-giving gift" (Romans 5:17 *Message*).

❝ SHe SAiD It ❞

Death is a Dialogue between
The Spirit and the Dust.
"Dissolve" says Death. —
The Spirit "Sir I have another Trust"—
Death doubts it—Argues from the Ground—
The Spirit turns away
Just laying off for evidence
An Overcoat of Clay.

EMILY DICKINSON

Paul insisted that *everyone* who places his or her faith in the **crucified** and risen Jesus Christ will receive eternal life. He preached a simple gospel: "Christ died for our sins, just as the Scriptures said. He was buried, and he was raised from the dead on the third day, as the Scriptures said" (1 Corinthians 15:3, 4). And he wrote, "Christ has rescued us from the curse . . . When he was hung on the cross, he took upon himself the curse for our wrongdoing" (Galatians 3:13).

Through His death and resurrection, Jesus not only gives eternal life to those who place their *trust* in Him, He also "crushed the head" of *Satan*, the evil one who enticed Eve to sin so long ago.

The Bible says Jesus willingly died on the *cross*: "For only by dying could he break the power of the *Devil*, who had the power of death. Only in this way could he deliver those who have lived all their lives as slaves to the fear of dying" (Hebrews 2:14-15).

God loves to make things new! The Big Crash has made this world old and decrepit, but God has promised to make "new heavens" and a "new earth" (2 Peter 3:13). He's so committed to this universe-wide project that He includes *you*. God has done in Jesus Christ everything necessary to provide you with a "new, life-giving way" to God (Hebrews 10:20). Through faith in Christ, you learn how to live in the "new way, by the Spirit" (Romans 7:6).

HiGH POiNtS in HiSToRY

One old tradition claims that John Chrysostom, bishop of Constantinople in the fifth century, got a summons to appear before the emperor. The ruler threatened him with banishment if he did renounce Jesus Christ.

"You cannot banish me," Chrysostom declared, "for my life is hid with Christ in God."

"Then I will take away your treasure," the emperor said.

"You cannot," the old Christian answered, "for my treasure is in heaven, where my heart is."

"Then I will drive you away from all your friends," the emperor threatened.

"You cannot," Chrysostom said, "for I have one friend from whom you can never separate me."

The exasperated emperor turned to his colleagues and asked, "What can you do with such a man?"

God has done everything necessary to allow you to enjoy life to the full.

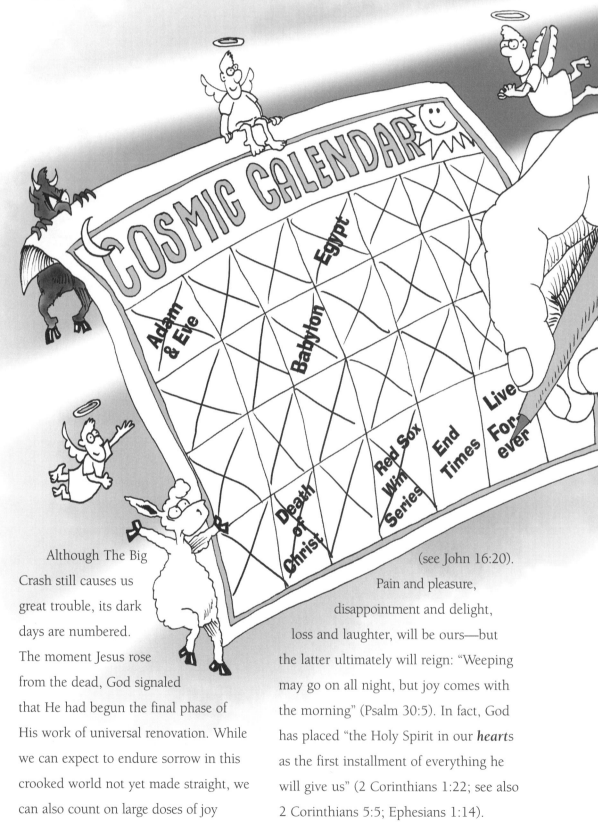

God promises to replace your sorrow with joy.

COSMIC CALENDAR

Adam & Eve

Babylon

Egypt

Death of Christ

Red Sox Win Series

End Times

Live For ever

Although The Big Crash still causes us great trouble, its dark days are numbered. The moment Jesus rose from the dead, God signaled that He had begun the final phase of His work of universal renovation. While we can expect to endure sorrow in this crooked world not yet made straight, we can also count on large doses of joy (see John 16:20). Pain and pleasure, disappointment and delight, loss and laughter, will be ours—but the latter ultimately will reign: "Weeping may go on all night, but joy comes with the morning" (Psalm 30:5). In fact, God has placed "the Holy Spirit in our *hearts* as the first installment of everything he will give us" (2 Corinthians 1:22; see also 2 Corinthians 5:5; Ephesians 1:14).

👉 So What?

👉 You should never expect to live completely free of pain and disappointment, because this world still suffers from The Big Crash.

👉 God wants to use your pain and heartache to remind you that you find life and wholeness only in Him.

👉 Pain and sorrow will give way to pleasure and joy for everyone who trusts in Jesus Christ.

SHeEP TaLK

Lord, our sin—*my* sin—has messed up this world pretty seriously. I admit that my failure to obey Your good commands has often hurt other people, hurt myself, and put up a barrier between You and me. But I am so happy and blessed to know that You took the initiative to make things right again, through the work of Your Son, Jesus Christ! Help me to commit myself and my life to You every day, so that every day really does get off on the right foot. In Jesus' name, Amen.

CHAPTER FOUR

A NeW Us

God refused to let the tragedy of The Big Crash ruin His plans to spend eternity with us. To live with us joyfully, however, He had to make us into people different from what we were. He had to remove our sin and give us new hearts eager to please Him. So what did He do? He made us into entirely new people: "Those who become Christians become new persons. They are not the same anymore, for the old life is gone. A new life has begun!" (2 Corinthians 5:17).

When we place our faith in Jesus and what He did for us through the cross, "we really have been changed into new and different people" (Galatians 6:15).

He SAiD It

"Be yourself" is about the worst advice you can give some people.

TOM MASSON

This radical change happens the moment we put our trust in Jesus—and yet as new people in Christ, we also have the opportunity to become more and more like Him every day. The apostle Paul declared, "We can be mirrors that brightly reflect the glory of the Lord" and then added "As the Spirit of the Lord works within us, *we become more and more like* him and reflect his glory even more" (2 Corinthians 3:18 emphasis added).

That means our becoming new people in Christ is both an event *and* a process.

❝ He SAiD It ❞

I am not what I ought to be,
what I want to be,
Not what I am going to be,
But thankful
That I am not what I used to be.

JOHN WOODEN

It's something like a rookie basketball player joining the NBA. The rookie is never more of an NBA player than he is at the moment he signs his contract. But through the years he can—and is expected to—become a more effective player, develop his skills, and increasingly contribute to the success of his team. His status as an NBA player doesn't change throughout his professional career, but the way he performs had better.

The QUeSTiON BoX

1. As you reflect the Lord's glory, is your mirror...
Cracked?
   Rippled?
      Cloudy?
         Smudged?
            Crystal clear?
2. What do you think it would take to polish your mirror so that it reflects God's glory as He wants it to?

ON THe WaY To THe NBA

Moments after he was drafted #2 in the 2004 NBA draft, University of Connecticut center Emeka Okafor answered a question from the press corps:

Q: Does being the No. 2 pick alleviate any pressure, as opposed to going No. 1?

Okafor: There's always pressure. No matter what pick, no matter when you're picked up, there's always pressure to perform. If anything, it's going to be even more pressure. You're the first pick of a franchise. So, there we go, right?[1]

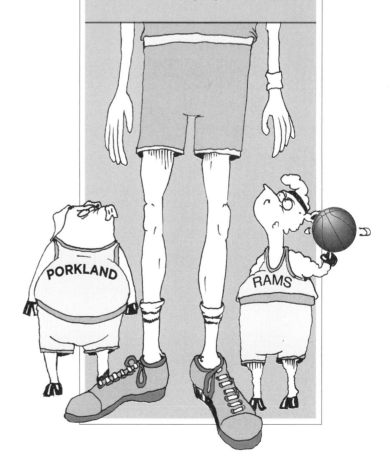

Most Christians really want to "perform" better than they did before they made a commitment to follow Christ. They know that sin and God don't mix, so they try very hard to sin less than they used to—and in so doing they make a terrible mistake.

Mistake? You bet, and a big one. The problem is, many try to *manage* their sin using all kinds of tricks rather than relying on God's power to radically transform them into new people. Worse yet, even if they appear to succeed for awhile in sinning less, they still feel like giant failures. They still think of themselves as anything but "new persons." They still feel dirty and imagine God sitting up in heaven, arms crossed, shaking His head and saying disapprovingly, "That's a bit better, kid—but still not good enough. Try again."

The truth is that no amount of discipline or tricks or will power can give us the ability to "manage" our sin effectively. Sin is not a pet; it can't be tamed or corralled through some kind of obedience training. Neither can it be ignored, for the Bible tells us, "Seek to live a clean and holy life, for those who are not holy will not see the Lord" (Hebrews 12:14).

Here's our dilemma: we might want to be *better* people, but God insists that we become *holy* people. In fact, He declares, "You *must* be holy because I am holy" (1 Peter 1:16, emphasis added). And how can we do *that?* The only way for us to become holy is to become more like Jesus. Not merely to *act* more like Jesus, but to *become* more like Him. And that requires transformation, not redecoration.

A GoOD NiGHT KiSS FoR TWiGGY?

An eighteen-year-old Englishman, Jordan Lazelle, had to be hospitalized after his pet scorpion bit him. One evening when Lazelle tried to give "Twiggy" its usual good-night kiss, the beast grabbed his lip. When Lazelle opened his mouth in shock, the scorpion jumped inside and stung him several times on the tongue. *Interesting*, you might be thinking, *but what does a stupid pet owner have to do with trying to deal with sin?* Plenty, it turns out. Christians who misunderstand and misuse God's grace tend to make the same kinds of painful mistakes committed by Jordan. They think they can make a pet out of a predator. Jordan chose a scorpion; many Christians choose sin. All of them mistakenly think that they can turn a wild and dangerous killer into a nice, little kitty or a sweet, playful doggy. And then, without warning, the thing sinks its fangs into their face.

God doesn't want us to sin *less* so much as He wants us to reflect Him *more*. He doesn't want remodeled hearts, but brand-new ones. He wants to give us a new set of spiritual taste buds, not put us on a restrictive diet plan. He wants us to crave new things, not to deny ourselves what we really like.

The apostle Paul once had to retrain some young Christian friends who forgot this crucial lesson. They started thinking that the key to a successful Christian life was straining hard to sin less. Paul told them, "Now it's wonderful if you are eager to do good"—can you sense the "but" coming?—"But oh, my dear children! I feel as if I am going through labor pains for you again, and they will continue *until Christ is fully developed in your lives*" (Galatians 4:18-19, emphasis added).

The goal is not to sin less on the outside; the goal is to allow Christ to grow on the inside.

This transformation starts in your mind and over time works its way outward to radically affect the way you use your body. "Don't copy the behavior and customs of this world," the Bible tells us, "but let God transform you into a new person by *changing the way you think*" (Romans 12:2, emphasis added).

And how do you start to change your thinking? The Bible answers, "Fix your thoughts on what is true and honorable and right. Think about things that are pure and lovely and admirable. Think about things that are excellent and worthy of praise" (Philippians 4:8). When you do, in time you see a remarkable transformation beginning to take shape in your life. When you think about Christ more than you think about sin, you find it increasingly possible to control your body and you start to crave what pleases God more than you used to desire what pleased only yourself.

A DaY SPa for YouR SouL

Since Christ grows in you as you focus on Him, try a little exercise to help you fix your mind on Him. Read and meditate on the highlighted passages, and then answer each question that follows.

John 8:31–36
What do you learn about truth in this passage?

John 5:19–30
What do you see that is honorable in this passage?

Matthew 11:16–19
What do you see that is right in this passage?

Hebrews 7:23–28
What looks pure in this passage?

Mark 14:3–9
What appears lovely in this passage?

Luke 4:16–22
What seems admirable in this passage?

Mark 7:31–37
What appears excellent in this passage?

Luke 2:25–35
What is worthy of praise in this passage?

SHe SAiD It

Any transition serious enough to alter your definition of self will require not just small adjustments in your way of living and thinking, but a full-on metamorphosis.

MARTHA BECK

You might already have guessed that this business of personal transformation depends on two people. Everything begins, of course, with God. (And if that weren't true, we'd all be in trouble.)

Our personal transformation is ultimately God's work. He makes it His business to see that we have all the resources we need to become more and more like Jesus. The apostle Paul writes, "I am sure that God, who began the good work within you, will continue his work until it is finally finished on that day when Christ Jesus comes back again" (Philippians 1:6). John adds, "Yes, dear friends, we are already God's children, and we can't even imagine what we will be like when Christ returns. But we do know that when he comes we will be like him, for we will see him as he really is" (1 John 3:2). God "is able to keep you from stumbling" and He will "bring you into his glorious presence innocent of sin and with great joy" (Jude 24).

God intends not only to transform our character; He promises to transform even our physical bodies! He promises that Jesus "will take these weak mortal bodies of ours and change them into glorious bodies like his own, using the same mighty power that he will use to conquer everything, everywhere" (Philippians 3:21). And when will this happen? The Bible answers, "For we know that when this earthly tent we live in is taken down—when we die and leave these bodies—we will have a home in *heaven*, an eternal body made for us by God himself and not by human hands" (2 Corinthians 5:1).

Why such an emphasis on new bodies? Because God isn't interested in asking us merely to manage sin. He insists on total transformation!

He SAiD It

The Christian ideal has not been tried and found wanting; it has been found difficult and left untried.

G. K. CHESTERTON

While we live and breathe on this earth, we also have an important part to play in our transformation. That's why Paul says, "I . . . beg you to lead a life worthy of your calling, for you have been called by God" (Ephesians 4:1).

SHe SAiD It

It's easy to follow when we want to go where the leader is taking us, but what about when He takes a turn we're not in favor of?

LISA BARRY

He wouldn't beg if it just happened automatically. He tells us, "You must live in a manner worthy of the Good News about Christ, as citizens of heaven" (Philippians 1:27). And he insists, "Those who claim they belong to the Lord must turn away from all wickedness" (2 Timothy 2:19).

Does this sound as if it takes effort? It does! Often it requires strenuous effort—but not the kind you might be imagining. The real work isn't trying to keep yourself from doing what you really want to do; it's more like changing your wardrobe. "Since you have heard all about him and have learned the truth that is in Jesus," Paul wrote, "throw off your old evil nature and your former way of life, which is rotten through and through, full of lust and deception. Instead, there must be a spiritual renewal of your thoughts and attitudes. You must display a new nature because you are a new person, created in God's likeness—righteous, holy, and true" (Ephesians 4:21-24). We are to "put to death the sinful, earthly things lurking within" and we must refuse to "lie to each other, for you have stripped off your old evil nature and all its wicked deeds. In its place you have clothed yourselves with a brand-new nature that is continually being renewed as you learn more and more about Christ, who created this new nature within you" (Colossians 3:5, 9-10).

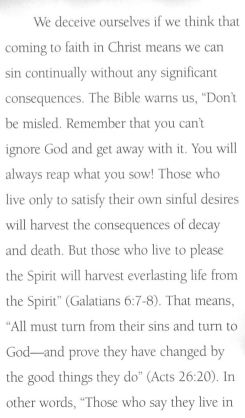

We deceive ourselves if we think that coming to faith in Christ means we can sin continually without any significant consequences. The Bible warns us, "Don't be misled. Remember that you can't ignore God and get away with it. You will always reap what you sow! Those who live only to satisfy their own sinful desires will harvest the consequences of decay and death. But those who live to please the Spirit will harvest everlasting life from the Spirit" (Galatians 6:7-8). That means, "All must turn from their sins and turn to God—and prove they have changed by the good things they do" (Acts 26:20). In other words, "Those who say they live in God should live their lives as Christ did" (1 John 2:6).

And how did Christ live? "I do nothing on my own," He said, "but I speak what the Father taught me. . . . For I always do those things that are pleasing to him" (John 8:28, 29). Jesus obeyed His Father and He expected His followers to imitate His example (see John 15:10). A few of His more halfhearted disciples somehow missed this truth and so Jesus asked them a pointed question: "Why do you call me 'Lord,' when you won't obey me?" (Luke 6:46).

Growing Christians take great delight in obeying God (see Romans 1:5; 16:26).

But you know what? The obedience God wants from us is not the "have to but don't want to" variety. It's instead the "need to and desire to" kind. God doesn't ask us to obey Him as we kick and scream; He wants us to obey Him as we skip and smile. And that takes a pretty amazing transformation.

God wants us to cooperate with His Spirit to transform us into men and women who eagerly desire to do His will. That, in fact, is a big part of why Jesus came to earth. Our **Savior** "gave himself for us to redeem us from all wickedness and to purify for himself a people that are his very own, *eager to do what is good*" (Titus 2:14 NIV, emphasis added).

🙶 He SAiD It 🙷

Cumpulsory obedience to a master is a state of slavery, willing obedience to one's father is the glory of sonship.

GANDHI

If we want to succeed in our spiritual lives, we have to make pleasing God our goal, *not* minimizing our sin. If we want to make God smile, we have to focus on loving Jesus, *not* on brute obedience. Remember, it was Jesus who said, "If you love me, you will obey what I command" (John 14:15 NIV). Love has to come before obedience; that's what makes the whole thing possible. And that kind of love requires a radical change of heart.

It all comes down to this: "Let the Lord Jesus Christ take control of you, and don't think of ways to indulge your evil desires" (Romans 13:14). Every moment of every day, invite Jesus Christ to live through you. And then watch the amazing things that start happening!

When we think about the transforming power of Christ in our lives, our thoughts can't help but lead us back to a fantastic word we've already considered: *glory.* Believers in Christ who choose to cooperate with the Spirit in the process of personal transformation can look forward to glory—and lots of it!

"God knew his people in advance," the Bible says, "and he chose them to become like his Son…. And having chosen them, he called them to come to him. And he gave them right standing with himself, and he promised them his glory" (Romans 8:29-30).

God has promised you His glory—and not just someday in heaven, but large chunks of it right now, right where you live.

☞ So What?

What happens when you choose to cooperate with God in the process of personal transformation? What do you gain?

☞ You feel great confidence and joy in the future (Romans 5:2).

☞ You do not have to fear God's coming judgment (Romans 5:9-10).

☞ You do not have to feel ashamed of yourself (1 John 2:28).

☞ You draw strength from tomorrow to find encouragement to face a difficult today (Romans 8:17-25).

☞ You can look forward to more than you can imagine (Romans 8:32).

SHeEP TaLK

Lord, above anything else, I want to become more and more like Jesus so that I can bring joy to Your heart and delight to my own. Help me to avoid falling into the trap of trying to "manage" my sin, and instead teach me to depend upon Your Spirit every moment to increasingly "form Christ" within me. Transform my mind, Lord, so that others can begin to see Your greatness in me. And I look forward to that wonderful day when I will see Jesus as He really is . . . and will be fully transformed into His likeness. Amen.

1. http://www.insidehoops.com/ndraftinterviews2.shtml

CHAPTER FIVE

CaTaLyST for CHaNGe

Sometimes we think it would be so much cooler if only we could live in the time of Jesus. To actually and physically walk and talk with Him, to see Him in His human body, right next to us; to hear Him speak and watch Him heal the crowds! We wonder if we wouldn't be better Christians if He actually lived right here, right now, as He did before.

But Jesus didn't think much of such an idea. In fact, He said it would be best for us if He went away (see John 16:7).

Best? How could that be?

It would be best, Jesus said, because if He did not go away, the Holy Spirit would not come. If He went away, however, He promised to send the Spirit not only to be *with* us (as Jesus was while on earth), but *in* us. And when that amazing event happened, we would be granted power to do even greater things than Jesus Himself did (see John 14:12).

He SAiD It

The church . . . for too long has followed Casper, the friendly ghost, instead of seeking the fire of the Holy Ghost.

FRANCIS FRANGIPANE

Jesus accomplished amazing things during His time on earth, not primarily because He was the Son of God, but because He depended completely on the Spirit—just as we can.

In fact, the Bible tells us that Jesus lived His whole life in submission to His Father's will and in dependence on the Spirit's power and leading.

Jesus went where He went because the Spirit led Him there (see Matthew 4:1). When Jesus preached, He spoke in the power of the Spirit (see Matthew 12:18; Luke 4:18). When He cast out demons, He did so through the power of the Spirit (see Matthew 12:28). When He traveled from place to place, He walked with the Spirit (see Luke 4:14). When He praised God with shouts of joy, He did so in the Spirit (see Luke 10:21). When He gave instructions for the future, He did so by the Spirit (see Acts 1:2). And even when He offered Himself as a sacrifice for our sins, He did so through the eternal Spirit (see Hebrews 9:14).

Jesus' whole earthly life, in fact, could be summed up like this: "Then Jesus, full of the Holy Spirit . . ." (Luke 4:1).

❝ He SAiD It ❞

Spell this out in capital letters: THE HOLY SPIRIT IS A PERSON. He is not enthusiasm. He is not courage. He is not energy. He is not the personification of all good qualities, like Jack Frost is the personification of cold weather. Actually, the Holy Spirit is not the personification of anything. . . . He has individuality. He is one being and not another. He has will and intelligence. He has hearing. He has knowledge and sympathy and ability to love and see and think. He can hear, speak, desire, grieve and rejoice. He is a Person.

A.W. TOZER

SoMeONE YoU SHoULD KNoW

Aiden Wilson Tozer (1897-1963) pastored several churches in the Christian and Missionary Alliance, served as editor of his denomination's *Alliance Life* magazine and authored more than forty books, at least two of which are still considered classics: *The Pursuit of God* and *The Knowledge of the Holy.* And he did all of this without ever receiving a formal theological education.

Tozer committed his life to Jesus Christ at age seventeen and took his first pastorate two years later. He never owned a car and instead relied on bus and train service for travel, even after he became well known. Throughout his life he gave a large portion of his royalties to people in need. He made the Christian faith come alive for untold numbers of believers who resonated with his passionate relationship with God. Historian Leonard Ravenhill once said about Tozer, "I fear that we shall never see another Tozer. Men like him are not college bred but Spirit taught."[1]

Jesus accomplished what He did by relying on the Spirit's power.

Would you like a quick picture of what it looks like to live "in the Spirit," as Jesus did? Would you like to see what can happen when you allow yourself to be ""full of the Spirit," like Jesus? Then consider what happened in the lives of Jesus' earliest followers. God performed many miracles through these Spirit-filled believers, such as healing people, casting out demons, and even bringing the dead back to life. But to be "filled with the Spirit" means a lot more than that.

❝ SHe SAiD It ❞

Trying to do the Lord's work in your own strength is the most confusing, exhausting, and tedious of all work. But when you are filled with the Holy Spirit, then the ministry of Jesus just flows out of you.

CORRIE TEN BOOM

Consider just a few things Jesus' first followers accomplished through their willing partnership with the Holy Spirit:

➤ They spoke boldly about their faith in Christ (Acts 1:8; 4:8, 31; 6:10).

➤ They spoke in languages they had never learned (Acts 2:4; 10:44-46).

➤ They received special instructions from God (Acts 8:29; 10:19; 13:2).

➤ They traveled from town to town (Acts 8:39).

➤ They felt great encouragement (Acts 9:31).

➤ They made accurate predictions about the future (Acts 11:28; 21:11).

➤ They received wisdom to make difficult judgments (Acts 15:28).

➤ They rose to positions of great leadership (Acts 20:28).

In short, they lived life to the fullest because they made it a habit to be "filled with the Spirit" (Acts 2:4; 4:8, 31; 6:3, 5; 7:55; 9:17; 11:24; 13:9, 52).

AND NoW, A WoRD FRoM GoD...

But you, dear friends, must continue to build your lives on the foundation of your holy faith. And continue to pray as you are directed by the Holy Spirit. Live in such a way that God's love can bless you as you wait for the eternal life that our Lord Jesus Christ in his mercy is going to give you.

JUDE 20-21

The earliest believers accomplished great things for God by relying on the Spirit's power.

And you know what? The same Holy Spirit who gave Jesus strength and direction is available to you! Remember what Jesus said: "It is actually best for you that I go away, because if I don't, the Counselor won't come. If I do go away, he will come because I will send him to you" (John 16:7).

Once Jesus returned to heaven, He sent the Spirit into the world, to do in us what He had been doing in Jesus. But not only that!

Now back in heaven, Jesus does something for us He could not have done while on earth. John tells us, "There is someone to plead for you *before the Father. He is Jesus Christ*, the one who pleases God completely" (1 John 2:1, emphasis added). At this very moment, Jesus is appearing before God to plead *your* case. In fact, the Bible says Jesus "lives forever to plead with God" on your behalf, as your perfect High Priest who "sat down in the place of highest honor in heaven, at God's right hand" (Hebrews 7:25; 8:1).

❝ SoMEoNe ❞ SaiD IT

Just as a strong wind will blow through an open window and stir things up in a house, so the Holy Spirit will blow new life into your life—if you give Him access.

U N K N O W N

Reasons to "Prosper" Believers

1.) Created in your image

2.) Glorifies your name

3.) [Go]d Golfers

4.) Some have a sense of humor; some "get it."

So the Spirit works *for* all of us and *in* all of us—at the same time, all over the world—*and* Jesus prays for all of us, also at the same time, all over the world.

And *that's* why you can do amazing things for God.

The QUeSTiON BoX

1. How would you describe your relationship with the Holy Spirit?

2. What prayers do you think Jesus is offering for you right now?

3. What "amazing things" have you done for God? What "amazing things" do you think you could do?

The Spirit will give you the ability to speak boldly and effectively, as God's friend, even in hostile situations (see Matthew 10:20). He will help you to remember crucial pieces of information at crucial times so that you can enjoy a successful Christian life (see John 14:26). He will give you both the desire and the ability to serve God with great joy (see Romans 7:6). He will strengthen you and make it possible for Jesus to live his life through you—something that delights God's heart (see Romans 8:4-5). And He will enable you to stop doing things that hurt yourself and sadden God (see Romans 8:13).

When you live in this way—when you ask God's Spirit to regularly fill you—then you set the stage for amazing things to take place. Don't forget that Jesus Himself told us, "The truth is, anyone who believes in me will do the same works I have done, *and even greater works,* because I am going to be with the Father" (John 14:12, emphasis added).

❝❝ He PRaYeD It ❞❞

O Holy Spirit, descend bountifully into my heart. Enlighten the dark corners of this neglected dwelling and scatter there Your cheerful beams.

ST. AUGUSTINE

WHaT KiND of GReaTeR WoRKS?

Jesus raised people from the dead, walked on water, fed thousands with practically nothing, healed multitudes, freed the demon-possessed, turned water into wine. So what kind of "greater works" did He have in mind for us (John 14:12)?

Perhaps a young boy named Joshua Sundquist could help answer that question.

When he was eight, doctors diagnosed Joshua with a fast-growing bone cancer and amputated his left leg; fifteen nauseating chemotherapy treatments followed. Yet Joshua could still say, "Whatever we're doing and whenever it is, God will be with us. That's why we don't need to be afraid."

Five years after the amputation, an older but still faithful Joshua declared, "God has blessed me very much. He has helped me to overcome and persevere through my problems. He will do the same for you if you trust Him and remember that circumstances don't last forever. But God does."

When you see God's Spirit building a rock-solid faith like this into a person's life, then you're seeing one of those "greater works."[2]

But how? *How* are we supposed to be "filled with the Spirit"? And how can we make it a habit to become full of the Spirit, as Jesus was?

Right off the bat, we notice that the Bible doesn't offer us a 1-2-3-step program to be filled with the Spirit. And be honest—doesn't that seem a little disappointing? Maybe even a little discouraging? Please, don't let it be, because it's not an oversight. Nor is it bad news. And here's why.

Since God doesn't give us a canned presentation on "how to be filled with the Spirit," that must mean that it is neither a complicated nor a difficult process. God doesn't leave our spiritual lives to chance, and He never overlooks anything crucial to our success. So what can we learn from the Bible about how to be filled with the Spirit?

We get a number of important clues from Ephesians 5:18, which says simply, "Don't be drunk with wine, because that will ruin your life. Instead, let the Holy Spirit fill and control you."

Clue 1: This is a divine command, an order. It is not a mere suggestion, a guideline, or a recommendation. That means it has to be *doable*.

Clue 2: The language of the original text (written in Greek) makes it clear that this is an ongoing action, a day-by-day and moment-by-moment activity, not a once-and-for-all event. That means it has to be *simple*.

Clue 3: The passage gives us only one illustration—a very unexpected one. Paul compares being filled with the Spirit to drinking wine. Now, why use such an apparently odd illustration?

89

Being filled with the Spirit is something like drinking wine.

❝ He SAiD It ❞

The problem is not that the churches
are filled with empty pews, but that the
pews are filled with empty people.

CHARLIE SHEDD

Paul declares that if we make it a habit to fill up on distilled spirits, we'll end up ruining our lives. But if instead we make it a habit to fill up on the Spirit of God, we'll end up enjoying the greatest lives possible. He uses the first picture to teach us something about a much greater spiritual reality. So what are the similarities—and differences—between the two? How does drinking wine give us a clue on how to be filled with the Spirit?

First similarity: in both cases, you have to choose to drink. If you don't make the choice to drink wine, then you don't get a single drop of alcohol. In the same way, if you don't choose to be filled with the Spirit, then your life will fill up with everything but Him. To make either happen, you have to make a conscious choice.

First dissimilarity: The choice to drink wine requires that you get filled up from an exterior source, quickly depleted. You have to go outside of yourself to lay your hands on some liquor.

The choice to be filled with the Spirit, however, requires that you drink from an inextinguishable resource flowing from *within* you, as Jesus said: "If you believe in me, come and drink! For the Scriptures declare that rivers of living water will flow out from within" (John 7:38). It's *much* simpler to do the latter than the former!

Yee-HAW!

A pastor got fed up with his congregation and so one Easter Sunday decided to skip services and instead go play golf. The apostle Peter looked down from heaven, saw the pastor on the golf course, and reported him to the Holy Spirit. Peter suggested that the Spirit severely punish the pastor. But as he continued to watch, Peter saw the pastor playing the best game he had ever played; he even got a hole-in-one on the toughest hole on the course. So Peter turned to the Spirit and asked, "I thought you were going to punish him. Do you call this punishment?" The Spirit replied, "Who can he tell?"

Second similarity: In both cases, you have to drink a lot. In the case of wine, you have to keep letting the alcohol slide down your throat; in that way, you make it a part of you. In the case of the Spirit, you must consciously and continuously invite Him to lead you, guide you, strengthen you, help you, and then let Him become a vital part of who you are. Whatever the situation, you reach out to God and say, "Dear Lord, please fill me with Your Spirit right now. Let me drink Him in!"

Second dissimilarity: When you fill up on wine, you lose control and very often end up caving in to your worst impulses and darkest instincts. On the other hand, when you invite the Spirit to fill you, you gain the kind of self-control that really amounts to God-control: "If the Holy Spirit controls your mind, there is life and peace" (Romans 8:6). So Paul writes, "I advise you to live according to your new life in the Holy Spirit. Then you won't be doing what your sinful nature craves" (Galatians 5:16).

❝ He SAiD It ❞

I myself do nothing. The Holy Spirit accomplishes all through me.

WILLIAM BLAKE

It really is as simple as that: choose to be filled with God's Spirit and then ask God to fill you, time after time, all throughout the day. Decide to drink, and then drink a lot.

Simple . . . but not necessarily easy!

The truth is you'll face all kinds of temptations and roadblocks that call for more than the simple guidance you've just received. So where do you get help in those tough situations? Do you have to buy the next book in the series, attend the expensive advanced seminar, bribe a pricey guru to reveal his deepest spiritual secrets?

Nah. Leave your checkbook and Visa card where they are. God wants us to learn from each other the nuts and bolts of the "how to"—especially from believers who have been walking with Him for a long time. That's why Paul can say, "I ask you to follow my example and do as I do" (1 Corinthians 4:16).

So don't look to a book or a seminar or an "expert" to teach you what God wants to show you through rubbing elbows with His people. In fact, that's such a huge part of your spiritual growth that it's worth a whole chapter all by itself—something we might call "The Growing Community."

Beats me.

So What?

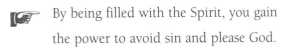

- By being filled with the Spirit, you gain the power to avoid sin and please God.

- By being filled with the Spirit, you experience the joy, peace, and satisfaction available only in God.

- By being filled with the Spirit, you can accomplish the kinds of things Jesus did—and even *more*.

He SAiD It

Churches don't need new members half so much as they need the old bunch made over.

BILLY SUNDAY

SHeEP TaLK

Lord, I really do want to be a better Christian, and I know that means I have to change. I also know that I can't change for the better without Your Spirit at work in me. So Lord, please fill me with Your Spirit right now, and show me those areas in my life that need to change. Give me the strength and the desire to please You and to gladly cooperate with Your Spirit as You work to form Jesus Christ in me. Help me to drink deeply and often of Your Spirit, so that I can be an effective coworker with You in what You want to accomplish on this earth. In Jesus' name I pray, amen.

1. http://www.worship.com/articlesbookslaw_tozer.htm
2. Dave and Jan Dravecky, *Portraits in Courage* (Grand Rapids, MI, Zondervan: 1998), 48, 49.

CHAPTER SIX

THe GRoWiNG CoMMuNiTY

In many circles today, the idea of *church* has fallen on hard times. People give all kinds of reasons for skipping it, but four in particular get a lot of airtime:

➤ "I just don't need it. I get along fine on my own."

➤ "I'm really not into organized religion."

➤ "I have no desire to hang around hypocrites."

➤ "I get enough church watching a Sunday morning service on TV."

While all four reasons have their problems, it's not hard to see how they've gained such popularity. The honest truth is that *nobody* needs church if all it amounts to is "come, sit, listen (a little), sleep (a little), give (a little), and go."

But that's *not* all church is. Not by a long shot.

❝ It SAiD It ❞

This is the gate of heaven. Enter ye all by this door. (This door is kept locked because of the draft. Please use the side entrance.)

SIGN HUNG ON
A CHURCH DOOR

God makes it very clear that He expects *every* growing believer to become an active part of a Christ-focused, dynamic local community of faith He calls "the church." He designed us to need each other and to help one another grow in faith. He never gives the tiniest hint in the Bible that He has *any* kind of growth plan for *any* believer in Jesus, other than the one He designed to work within the church.

All through the **New Testament**, God assumes His people will regularly meet together to worship and to encourage one another. So we constantly read phrases like this: "When you meet as a church" and "When you come together" and "When you gather for the **Lord's Supper**" (1 Corinthians 11:18, 20, 33).

God also explicitly commands us to gather as a church—and then explains why He gives the command. God thinks of all believers, together, as the "body of Christ," and so the Bible says, "We are all parts of his one body, and each of us has different work to do. And since we are all one body in Christ, we belong to each other, and each of us needs all the others" (Romans 12:5; see also 1 Corinthians 12:27). We *all* have work to do. We *all* belong to each other. We *all* need each other; nobody gets left out.

This means that if we choose not to get involved in a good local church, then either we are calling God a liar—we don't really need each other, when He says we do—or we're flatly telling Him, "I know better than You. Go jump in a lake." Do you suppose either option ever results in genuine spiritual growth?

A growing Christian finds great joy in obeying God—and the fact is that we can't obey literally *dozens* of biblical commands without remaining in close, regular contact with other believers. Consider just a few:

➤ *Encouraging each other* (Hebrews 10:25).

➤ *Loving each other* (John 13:34-35).

➤ *Forgiving each other* (Ephesians 4:32).

➤ *Building up each other* (1 Thessalonians 5:11).

➤ *Worshiping with each other* (Hebrews 12:28).

➤ *Warning each other* (Hebrews 3:13).

➤ *Serving each other* (Galatians 5:13).

None of us can claim to be "a good Christian" if we deliberately disobey commands like these. And we can't help but disobey them if we don't get plugged into a good local church.

He SAiD It

Love to Christ is proved by doing the things which he commands, and not merely saying, "Lord, Lord."

CHARLES HENRY
MACKINTOSH

You can't obey scores of God's commands without regular involvement in a local church.

God designed the church, in part, to fill a relationship void that can't be filled anywhere else.

One time Jesus was addressing a crowd when His mother and brothers showed up, seeking to speak with Him. "Who is my mother? Who are my brothers?" Jesus asked. Then He pointed to His disciples and said, "These are my mother and brothers. Anyone who does the will of my Father in heaven is my brother and sister and mother!" (Matthew 12:48-50).

Jesus felt closer to men and women in the church, at least in some ways, than He did to His own flesh and blood. And He wanted these friends to see each other in the same way.

❝ It SAiD It ❞

Don't wait for six strong men to carry you to church.

A CHURCH MARQUEE

At another time, *Peter* blurted out that he and the other disciples had "given up everything" to follow Jesus. Jesus replied, "I assure you that everyone who has given up house or brothers or sisters or mother or father or children or property, for my sake and for the Good News, will receive now in return, a hundred times over, houses, brothers, sisters, mothers, children, and property" (Mark 10:28-30). In the church, God gives us relationship riches far beyond anything we might enjoy in our biological families.

That's why the book of Acts uses the word "brothers" almost fifty times to describe fellow believers in Christ. And it's why early Christian leaders so often wrote the phrase "whom I love" to describe their church friends (see Romans 16:8; 1 Corinthians 4:17; Philippians 4:1; 2 John 1:1; 3 John 1:1).

❝SHe SAiD It❞

If my church experience is based upon what they are doing for me, and not what I can do, then pass the popcorn and start bringing Red Vines.

BRIDGET WILLARD

YoU PiCK tHe pHoNy

The Christian satirical magazine **The Door** loves to poke fun at the church "with the hope that our prodding might generate some course corrections while inducing a laugh or two . . . or three" (**www.thedoormagazine.com**). Four of the following five advertisements were featured in a *Door* regular feature called, "Truth Is Stranger Than Fiction." Can you spot the impostor?

➤ SORRY FOR SIN? Repent, 1-900-7REPENT, $3 first minute, $1 additional minute, must be 18, Fishnet Ministries.

➤ Be a witness to your loved ones and friends! Wear a RAPTURE WATCH!

➤ 03 Temple Cleanser. The most effective colon cleanser on the market!

➤ Prayer panties — Jesus' secret.

➤ Scratch 'n Sniff Bible: With one whiff, make the story of Lazarus rising from the dead COME ALIVE!!

In a vibrant church, we learn things about God and His will for us that we won't learn anywhere else. That means that if you avoid church because of its problems, then you forfeit great understanding about your heavenly Father and His ways.

Did you know that many books in the New Testament were written to churches *because* of some error they were committing or problem they were having? Some members of one local church thought they could perfect God's

work in them through self-effort; God took the opportunity to teach them about faith (see the book of Galatians). Some members of another church got all confused about Judgment Day; God took the opportunity to teach them about the return of Christ (see the books of 1 and 2 Thessalonians). Some members of a third local church took all kinds of theological wrong turns; God took the opportunity to teach them about His desire for unity and proper conduct and the wise use of spiritual gifts (see the books of 1 and 2 Corinthians).

If God's people in these places had neglected to regularly meet together, we wouldn't know nearly as much about God and His ways as we do. In fact, problems still drive us to God, forcing us to learn new things about Him.

God usually teaches us the most crucial lessons regarding our Christian life as we interact with others in the church. Did you know that this is exactly what the apostle Paul *pray*ed for? He wrote, "We ask God to give you a complete understanding of what he wants to do in your lives, and we ask him to make you wise with spiritual wisdom. Then the way you live will always honor and please the Lord, and you will continually do good, kind things for others. All the while, you will learn to know God better and better" (Colossians 1:9-10). All those "you"s are in the plural in the original Greek.

Paul did not pray that individual believers might receive divine wisdom to enable them to live solitary Christian lives. Instead, he prayed that his fellow Christians in the church might grow *together* in godly wisdom and so *together* come to know God better than ever. It's a prayer God still answers.

ANSWeR to You PiCK the PHoNY

No one, thank the Lord, has ever gotten a whiff of the Scratch 'n Sniff Bible.

ROUND UP

In the church you receive crucial instruction found nowhere else.

If you avoid church because you don't think you need it, or because you dislike organized religion, or for any other reason, then you also forfeit great understanding about yourself.

It was *in the church* that the apostle Paul discovered God had equipped him and called him to be a worldwide evangelist (see Acts 13:2).

It was *in the church* that Silas learned God had entrusted to him a crucial mission and where he became a close friend of Paul (see Acts 15:22).

It was *in the church* that Timothy learned God had called him to be a pastor and where he discovered both his greatest strengths and weaknesses (1 Timothy 4:14).

CaTCHiNG SoMe Zzzz'S?

Have you ever slept in church? Do you know someone who does? Then maybe you can relate to the following.

• As the students of a Sunday school teacher began to make their way to the church service, she asked them, "And why is it necessary to be quiet in church?" One honest little girl answered, "Because people are sleeping."

• One anonymous pundit said, "If all the people who fall asleep in church were laid end to end, they would be much more comfortable."

• And the late Vance Havner once declared, "Too many church services start at eleven sharp and end at twelve dull."

Okay, so some people in church may tick you off—but who knows whether they aren't *exactly* the people God has put in your life for a reason?

Also, how many kooky, bizarre, and even destructive things that individual Christians do could be avoided if only they would take seriously God's instruction about the church? God loves to give us guidance through the assembled church, something the early church understood well.

When a critical decision had to be made that would affect believers worldwide, the early church called a council of its leaders and sought God's direction. At the end of their meeting, they released a letter that said, "So it seemed good to us, having unanimously agreed on our decision . . . For it seemed good to the Holy Spirit and to us" (Acts 15:25, 28). The Holy Spirit led these early believers to make an important decision *together*.

If you think God is telling you to do something—especially if it's something unusual—one of the best ways to test your idea is to submit it for validation to the leadership of your local church. But how can you do that if you're not involved in a local church?

> Make pigs clean up after themselves after service.
> Anonymous

> Make cows go last at potlucks! They already have 2 stomachs.
> Anonymous

❝❝ SoMeoNe ❞❞ SAiD iT

One of the most difficult and challenging responsibilities of a Christian is holding his brothers and sisters in Christ accountable. God has not left us here as Lone Rangers, but He has give us a family to support and strengthen us. It is often impossible for us to be built up in our walk with Christ until the rubble of sin and disobedience has been cleared away. As a family, we must aid each other not only in the building, but also in clearing the rubble.

UNKNOWN

God has designed us so that we become more like Christ only when we remain in vital relationships with other Christians. We just don't grow spiritually when we try to go it alone.

Why not? Proverbs 27:17 explains: "As iron sharpens iron, a friend sharpens a friend." If you want to remain spiritually dull your whole life, then don't bother with church. But if you want to become a finely honed tool in the hands of God, then you have no choice but to place yourself in the company of other pieces of divinely forged iron in the church Jesus is building.

Greener Grass Church

Today's Sermon: 9:45 a.m.
"When the World Pulls the Wool over Your Eyes."

Today-12 p.m.
"Sheepkeepers" Shepherds' Support Group.

Little Lambs – 2 p.m.

Bright side of Barbed-wire Discussion – 6 p.m.

Think about this for a moment: What do all mature Christians most want to do with their lives? What one thing do strong believers count as more important to them than anything else in the universe? They want to glorify God. They want their lives to bring the Lord great praise.

And where do Christians best bring their Lord such glory? In the church: "Now glory be to God! By his mighty power at work within us, he is able to accomplish infinitely more than we would ever dare to ask or hope. May he be given glory *in the church* and in Christ Jesus forever and ever through endless ages. Amen" (Ephesians 3:20-21, emphasis added).

Do you want to bring great glory to God through your life? If you do, the best place for that to happen is in church.

JuST WHaT THe DoCToR ORDeReD

Many recent studies show that show church attendees tend to have lower blood pressure rates and only half the risk of heart attacks as those who do not regularly attend church. Regular participation in a faith community can also provide many other health benefits:

➤ A sense of meaning and purpose.

➤ A framework for setting priorities.

➤ A way to place stresses and crises in perspective.

➤ Comfort during illness or crisis.

➤ Support for a healthy lifestyle .

➤ Diminished suicide risk.

You grow more like Christ and bring Him glory only when you you remain closely connected to other growing believers.

Have you ever wondered why the Bible doesn't seem to give us an abundance of detailed instructions on the particulars of how to grow in faith? You won't find a comprehensive manual in the New Testament on how to pray, for example, or how to lead or how to minister to the sick or how to take communion or how to teach a class or how to deliver (or even listen to) a sermon. Why not?

It's because God wants us to learn many of the "how tos" of our faith in community, by rubbing shoulders and elbows with other believers who, perhaps, have walked with the Lord longer than we have.

We can trace this "learn by example" method all the way back to Jesus. When He washed the feet of His disciples before what we call "The Last Supper," He told them, "I have given you an example to follow. Do as I have done to you" (John 13:15). Years later, in describing how he used hard personal choices and life circumstances to lead people to a relationship with Christ, the apostle Paul said, "You should follow my example, just as I follow Christ's" (1 Corinthians 11:1). And Paul told some other Christian friends, "Pattern your lives after mine, and learn from those who follow our example" (Philippians 3:17).

Peter likewise told a group of pastors to lead "by your good example" (1 Peter 5:3), while another writer advised some Christian friends to carefully watch their leaders and to think "of all the good that has come from their lives, and trust the Lord as they do" (Hebrews 13:7).

God also instructs older Christian women to "train" younger women in how to love their husbands and children and how to take care of their homes (Titus 2:4-5). We are to learn by example!

👀 He SalD IT 👀

The Christian is not one who has gone all the way with Christ. None of us has. The Christian is one who has found the right road.

CHARLES L. ALLEN

The surest steps to happiness are the steps to church.

God molds you and shapes you by giving you living examples to follow.

If so far in your Christian life you've mostly attended church without getting too deeply involved—you could describe yourself as more the "scamper in and scoot out" kind of believer—then determine today to change your habits and investigate where you might plug in more fully to your church.

And if to this point you haven't had much to do with church, then ask the Lord to help you adjust your thinking to get more in line with His. Start looking around for a solid church that can help you get to know God better and start enjoying life as He intended.

So What?

- By getting involved at church, you learn important things about God and yourself that you won't learn anywhere else.

- By getting involved at church, you participate in God's *only* plan to help you grow spiritually.

- By getting involved at church, you find encouragement, love, strength, forgiveness, wisdom, and the motivation to keep drawing close to God.

He SAiD It

Church attendance is as vital to a believer as a transfusion of rich, healthy blood to a sick man.

DWIGHT L. MOODY

SHeEP TaLK

Lord, I want to live in a way that pleases You and gives You glory. So if You say that I can become that kind of person only by regularly rubbing shoulders with fellow believers in a church that honors Christ and takes seriously His Word, then I want to get involved. Please show me where I "fit" and help me to be an encouragement and a help to others, just as they encourage and help me. In Jesus' name I pray, amen.

THe GUiDeBooK

f you want to experience some fantastic place you've never before visited, you could do worse than prepare for your trip by studying a reputable guidebook. Through a good guidebook, you learn a lot about what and what not to do, where and where not to go, when and when not to visit, how and how not to get around.

In many ways—and in far more important ways than a vacation guide—the Bible is our indispensable Guidebook for a successful journey of faith. In fact, God designed it to give us the best experience possible.

He SAiD It

With a good guidebook, you can come into Paris for your first time, go anywhere in town for the equivalent of a dollar on the subway, enjoy a memorable bistro lunch for $10, and pay just $60 for a double room in a friendly hotel on a pedestrian-only street a few blocks from the Eiffel Tower—so French, that when you step outside in the morning you feel you must have been a poodle in a previous life. All you need is a good guidebook covering your destination.

RICK STEVES

Why should we think of the Bible as our Guidebook for a successful life of faith?

For one reason, that's how the Bible presents itself. None of us can do without the Bible's supernatural direction. So the psalmist prayed, "Guide my steps by your word, so I will not be overcome by any evil" (Psalm 119:133). *God's Word* directs our spiritual walk and guides us away from trouble.

God also tells us that His "people need more than bread for their life; real life comes by feeding on every word of the LORD" (Deuteronomy 8:3). The Bible is that "word of the LORD" and serves as our essential guide to life; if we want to grow, we have to feed on it daily. Jesus Himself quoted this verse and insisted that people "must feed on every word of God" (Matthew 4:4).

If you want to grow in your faith, you can't do without the spiritual food the Bible provides.

"...feed on it daily..."

❝ He SAiD It ❞

I prefer to believe those writers who get their throats cut for what they write.

BLAISE PASCAL

Godly individuals throughout history have used the Bible as their Guidebook for growing closer to God. *Israel*'s kings were commanded to copy the whole thing in their own handwriting, so they would become intimately familiar with it (see sidebar). God told Joshua, the successor to *Moses*, to "study this Book of the Law continually. Meditate on it day and night so you may be sure to obey all that is written in it. Only then will you succeed" (Joshua 1:8). When some conflict or question arose in Jesus' presence, He habitually appealed to the Guidebook by saying, "It is written" (Matthew 4:4, 7, 10; 11:10; 21:13; 26:24, 31, etc. NIV). And when some young Christians wanted to see if the apostle Paul had given them correct spiritual directions, "they searched the Scriptures day after day to check up on Paul and Silas, to see if they were really teaching the truth" (Acts 17:11).

A RoYaL HaNDWRiTiNG EXeRCiSe

Long before the nation existed, God instructed Israel about her future kings:

When he sits on the throne as king, he must copy these laws on a scroll for himself in the presence of the Levitical priests. He must always keep this copy of the law with him and read it daily as long as he lives. That way he will learn to fear the LORD his God by obeying all the terms of this law. This regular reading will prevent him from becoming proud and acting as if he is above his fellow citizens. It will also prevent him from turning away from these commands in the smallest way. This will ensure that he and his descendants will reign for many generations in Israel.

DEUTERONOMY 17:18-20

What qualifies the Bible to be called "the Guidebook"? What sets it apart? Why should it—and it alone—be called "God's Word"?

The Bible is different from *all* other books; nothing else is like it or even remotely equivalent to it. There may be all kinds of "holy books" in the world, and there may be countless books that inspire us and make us think, but only the Bible—the *Old and New Testaments*, together—deserves the name "the Word of God."

Centuries ago, when some alleged prophets said they spoke for God, the Lord answered through the prophet Jeremiah, "'Let these false prophets tell their dreams, but let my true messengers faithfully proclaim my every word. There is a difference between chaff and wheat! Does not my word burn like fire?' asks the LORD. 'Is it not like a mighty hammer that smashes rocks to pieces?'" (Jeremiah 23:28-29).

God's words are not like those of anyone else. His words, like wheat, give life. His words, like fire, burn into the soul to clear away everything dead and rotting. His words, like a hammer, break all opposition and create fertile soil where His Word can take root and grow. God says of His Word, "I send it out, and it always produces fruit. It will accomplish all I want it to, and it will prosper everywhere I send it" (Isaiah 55:11).

It'S aLL aLoNe

Are all "holy books" essentially the same? Not according to Professor M. Monier-Williams (1819-1899), a Boden professor of Sanskrit at Oxford. He was born in Bombay, India, and spent forty-two years studying Eastern religious books. Toward the end of his career he wrote the following:

Pile them, if you will, on the left side of your study table; but place your own Holy Bible on the right side—all by itself, all alone—and with a wide gap between them. For . . . there is a gulf between it and the so-called sacred books of the East which severs the one from the other utterly, hopelessly, and forever . . . a veritable gulf which cannot be bridged over by any science or religious thought.[1]

What makes the Bible so different? First, it is inspired by God in a way unlike any other book (see 2 Timothy 3:16). Somehow, the Holy Spirit "moved the prophets to speak from God" (2 Peter 1:21). Even though men spoke these words, the real source was God. So Paul can say, "The Holy Spirit was right when he said to our ancestors through Isaiah the prophet . . . " (Acts 28:25). When the Bible speaks, it is God speaking (see Hebrews 3:7; 10:15).

Second, the Bible speaks truth into your soul, cutting to the very core of your being: "For the word of God is full of living power. It is sharper than the sharpest knife, cutting deep into our innermost thoughts and desires. It exposes us for what we really are" (Hebrews 4:12).

Third, God scattered hundreds of prophecies throughout His book to assure us of its divine Source. To demonstrate the total trustworthiness of His book—and to prove the identity of His Son—God fulfilled more than a hundred specific Bible predictions in the life of Jesus, all of them given hundreds of years before Christ's birth.

If King James was good enough for Paul, then it's good enough for me.

Many critics claim that the Bible can't be trusted, that it's no different from any other book, that it's full of errors and ancient myths. But don't ever bet against the Bible! It has a long record of besting its critics.

He SAiD It

I am busily engaged in the study of the Bible. I believe it is God's word because it finds me where I am.

ABRAHAM LINCOLN

In an online advertisement, a popular publication called itself "The entertainment Bible" and asked, "Wouldn't you rather have *this* in your hotel room?" If you really want to grow as a Christian, the answer is no. Why? Because the Bible can do for you what no other book or publication can. Consider just six of the tremendous benefits God designed the Bible to give you.

1. Spiritual strength

By reading the Bible and applying its wisdom, you receive great encouragement, the ability to endure in tough times, and an unflinching hope (see Romans 15:4). A daily meal of God's Word makes you strong spiritually.

2. Spiritual discernment

By regularly wading into the life-giving waters of the Bible, you develop the ability to discern what is best for you and learn how to live what the Bible calls a "blameless" life (Philippians 1:9-11).

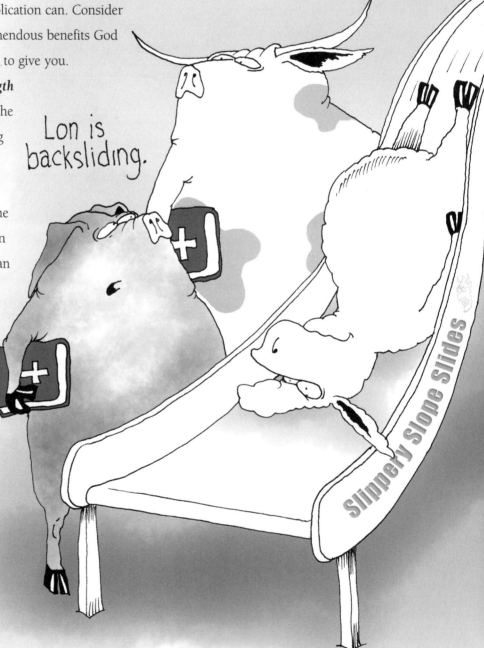

Lon is backsliding.

Slippery Slope Slides

3. Spiritual growth

The Bible teaches us all kinds of crucial things necessary for our spiritual growth. It rebukes us and corrects us when we get off track. And it trains us and equips us for a life worth living, one that receives God's enthusiastic praise (see 2 Timothy 3:16).

4. Knowledge of God

The Bible gives us thrilling knowledge about God the Father and His Son, Jesus Christ, that we won't get anywhere else. That knowledge allows us to share in God's divine nature and to escape the corruption all around us (see 2 Peter 1:3-4).

5. Close relationship with God

The Bible tells us what we need to know about how to develop and enjoy a fulfilling relationship with God, both now and for eternity (see 2 Timothy 3:15).

6. Crucial warnings

The Bible warns us away from dangerous theological errors, foolish lifestyle decisions that would ruin us, and all kinds of back alleys and dead ends that would keep us from growing spiritually (see 1 Corinthians 10:6-11).

The words of an ancient wise man still hold true today: "Hold on to instruction, do not let it go; guard it well, for it is your life" (Proverbs 4:13 NIV).

Yee-HAW!

"The art of prophecy is very difficult, especially with respect to the future," one wag once said, and with good reason. While the Bible is still batting 1.000 on its many hundreds of prophecies, others have not fared so well. Consider a few failed prophecies from modern times:

"Heavier-than-air flying machines are impossible."
Lord Kelvin, president, Royal Society, 1895

"There is no reason anyone would want a computer in their home."
Ken Olson, president, chairman, and founder of Digital Equipment Corp., 1977

"We don't like their sound, and guitar music is on the way out."
Decca Recording Co., rejecting the Beatles, 1962

"640K ought to be enough for anybody."
Bill Gates, 1981

It has always been important for people to be able to read the Bible in their own language. The Old Testament, written mostly in Hebrew (with a few small portions in Aramaic, a related language), was translated into Greek about two centuries before Christ, in order to serve the needs of Greek-speaking Jews living outside of Palestine. The New Testament was written in Greek, the international language of the first century.

But by the fourth century, far more people spoke Latin—and so a brilliant scholar named Jerome translated the whole Bible into Latin. His version is commonly called "The Vulgate." Later, other translations were needed:

John Wycliffe's followers translated the Bible into English from the Vulgate (c. 1380).

William Tyndale translated the New Testament into English, using the original Greek texts (1525).

Martin Luther translated the entire Bible into German (1534).

Matthew's Gospel was translated into Malay, the first non-European language version (1629)

The Bible was translated for Massachusetts native Americans (1662).

By 1800, portions of the Bible were available in sixty-six languages and the complete Bible available in forty languages

Today, portions of the Bible are available in more than two thousand languages, with the complete Bible available in about five hundred languages.[2]

As amazing as the Bible is, it won't do you or anyone else any good if it just lies around on a table or stays shelved on a dusty bookcase. It's like a treasure chest: to benefit from what's inside, you have to open it and get at its gleaming contents. And how can you best do that?

➤ *Make a regular meal out of it.*

God compares taking time to digest the spiritual food of the Bible with taking time to digest healthy meals of ordinary food. You can't grow without either one. So He tells us, "You must crave pure spiritual milk so that you can grow into the fullness of your salvation. Cry out for this nourishment as a baby cries for milk, now that you have had a taste of the Lord's kindness" (1 Peter 2:2-3). Find and use a plan to read healthy portions of the Bible every day.

𝟞𝟞 SoMeONe 𝟫𝟫 SAiD It

The Bible is bread for daily use, not cake for special occasions.

ANONYMOUS

➤ *Take time throughout the day to ponder what you read, especially any portion that really hit home.*

Think about it. Meditate on it. Ask yourself, *What is God saying here? What does He want me to do? What might He want me to change?* Try a little exercise. Turn to Psalm 119, near the middle of your Bible. Read verses 15, 23, 27, 48, 78, 97, 99, and 148. What do you learn about meditating on God's Word? How can you benefit from it?

➤ *Cement portions of God's Word in your mind by memorizing them.*

Has a verse especially captured your attention? Then lock it away in the vault of your brain so that you can retrieve it whenever you need to. One ancient believer wisely told God, "I have hidden your word in my heart, that I might not sin against you" (Psalm 119:11). It's a great practice . . . and it *works!*

"O come with me to the Word of God!" urges contemporary author John Piper. "Whatever it costs, do not read it and leave it. It transforms us by its presence in our minds, not by staying on the bedside table."[3]

Tonight we feast on a prime cut of grade-A Gospel with Proverbs tips...

Save a Psalm for me!

Any good thing can get corrupted, and that's true of the way we use the Bible, too. So consider a few things to avoid in your reading and use of God's Word.

➤ *Never learn facts about the Bible or read and study it merely to gain additional religious knowledge.*

God speaks to us through the Bible to change *us*, to guide *us*, to correct *us*. He gave us the Bible so that we could "grow in the grace and knowledge of our Lord and Savior Jesus Christ" (2 Peter 3:18 NIV), not so that we could win quiz shows or impress others with how much we know. Jesus once told some religious leaders who prided themselves on their knowledge of the Bible, "You search the Scriptures because you believe they give you eternal life. But the Scriptures point to me! Yet you refuse to come to me so that I can give you this eternal life" (John 5:39-40).

➤ *Don't go beyond what the Bible actually instructs.*

We sometimes get ourselves into trouble by getting attached to some pet idea (usually something we "discovered") or getting enthralled with this or that set of teachings, and we give those things more authority than we do the Bible itself. But the Bible warns us, "Do not go beyond what is written" (1 Corinthians 4:6 NIV).

It's okay to develop personal convictions on issues not specifically addressed in God's Word, but you are to keep these convictions "between yourself and God" (Romans 14:22). Don't try to force them on others!

➤ *Don't consider the Bible's many promises as "lucky charms" to keep you always warm and comfortable.*

The devil loves to try to get believers to do exactly this. He even tried it with Jesus. He tempted Jesus to consider God's promise in Psalm 91 as a lucky charm—and Jesus refused to bite. Read Psalm 91 sometime and compare it with Matthew 4:5-7 to see if you can learn what error the devil made and how Jesus responded to it.

WeLL, I'LL Be

A ten-year-old boy proudly told his father, "I finally know what the Bible means!"

The boy's surprised father replied, "What do you mean, you 'know' what the Bible means? What does it mean, then?"

"That's easy, Dad," the boy replied. "It stands for Basic Instruction Before Leaving Earth!"

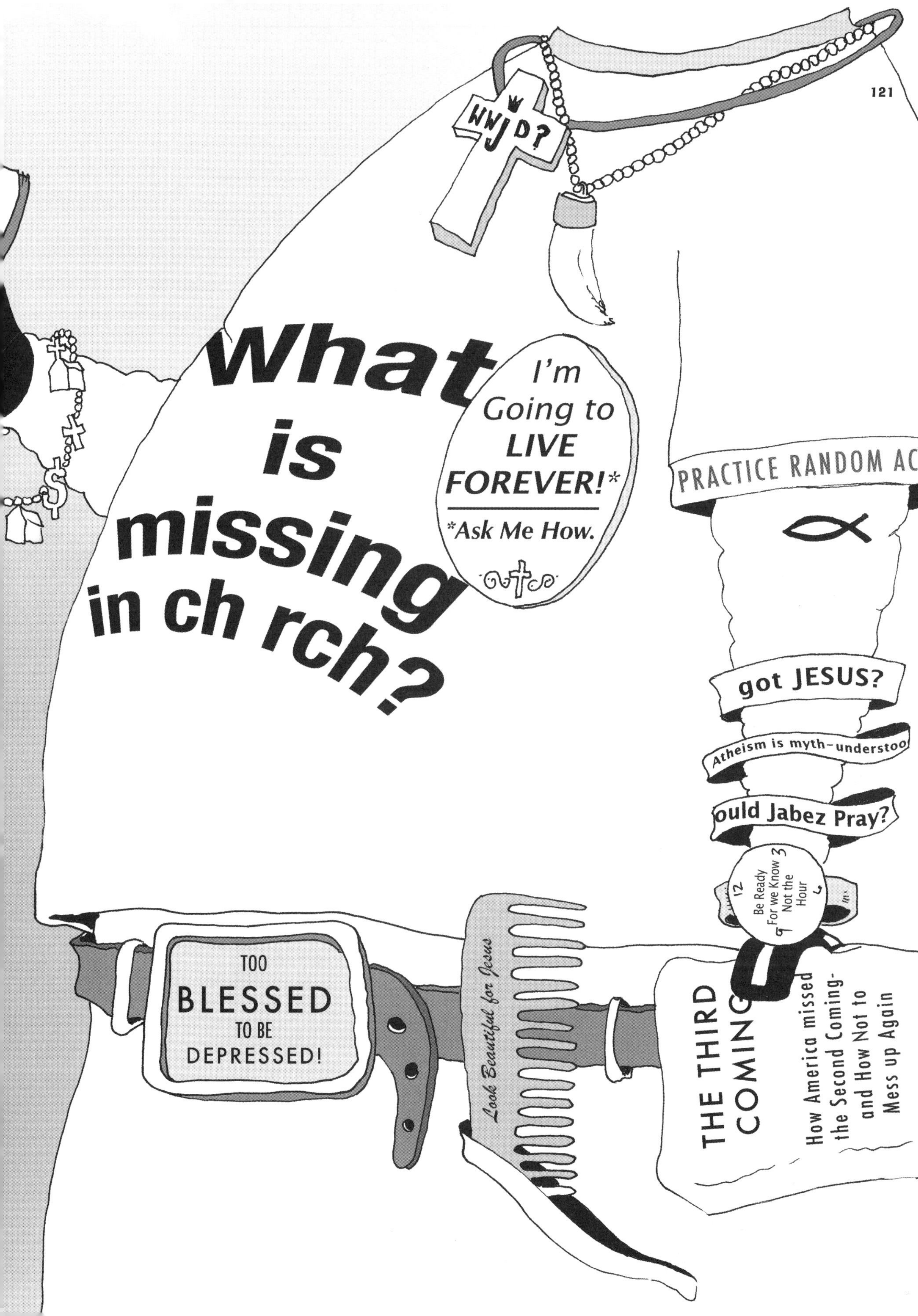

WWJD?

What is missing in ch rch?

I'm Going to **LIVE FOREVER!***

*Ask Me How.

PRACTICE RANDOM ACT

got JESUS?

Atheism is myth–understoo

ould Jabez Pray?

12 Be Ready For we Know Not the Hour

THE THIRD COMING

How America missed the Second Coming- and How Not to Mess up Again

TOO **BLESSED** TO BE DEPRESSED!

Look Beautiful for Jesus

As you become immersed in the world and wisdom of the Bible, never allow yourself to drift from the most important goal: our real mission as growing Christians is *always* to please God by joyfully obeying what He tells us, *not* merely to understand what we find in His Word. When one starstruck woman cried out to Jesus, "God bless your mother!" Jesus replied, "But even more blessed are all who hear the word of God and put it into practice" (Luke 11:27, 28).

The book of Romans is probably the most challenging portion of the whole New Testament. Yet at its core, it's very simple. As he began his book, Paul explained that he wrote so that people everywhere "will believe and obey" God, and so bring "glory to his name" (Romans 1:5). And as the book winds to a close, he reminds his readers that the gospel goes out to the whole world, "so that they might believe and obey Christ" (Romans 16:26). *That's* the goal.

Did you know that Bible study can be hazardous to your health? It can be, if you approach it in the wrong way.

If you go to God's Word merely to gain knowledge, or out of a grumbling sense of duty, but without the least spark of desire to have Him speak into your life—whether for encouragement or correction—then you could be heading for big trouble. Read Luke 12:35-48 if you want a healthy jolt of divine reality.

Do you really want to hear from God? Do you genuinely want to grow as a Christian? Do you honestly want to understand what God says to you in His Word? If so, then make it your habit to obey what you already understand in the Bible by relying on the power of the Spirit (see John 8:31-32; 7:17).

ROUTE 666 HWY TO HELL

Paved with Good Intentions

THeY SAiD It

The ship that will not obey the helm will have to obey the rocks.

ENGLISH PROVERB

At the end of the little book of Ephesians, God gives us some very helpful guidance on how to "be strong" as believers and how to "stand firm against all strategies and tricks of the Devil" (6:10-11). He uses the picture of human warfare to show us the very serious nature of spiritual growth.

"Put on salvation as your helmet," He tells us, "and *take the sword of the Spirit, which is the word of God*" (Ephesians 6:17, emphasis added). Since spiritual growth is a kind of war, you can never succeed without a divine weapon. And that weapon is a sword, the Bible.

☞ So What?

☞ Using the Bible wisely will guide you into the most satisfying life possible.

☞ You cannot benefit from the Bible's amazing riches without regularly mining its wisdom.

☞ The goal of all Bible reading and study is joyful obedience to God, not merely to amass Bible knowledge.

👀 He SAiD It 👀

When you have read the Bible, you know it is the Word of God, because it is the key to your heart, your own happiness, and your own duty.

FORMER PRESIDENT,
WOODROW WILSON

SHeEP TaLK

Lord, I am so thankful that in the Bible You have given me a completely reliable Guidebook that I can use to successfully navigate my entire life. Please help me to make a daily meal out of it and to remember that it is You speaking directly to my heart. Give me the strength and the desire to eagerly obey what I hear You telling me, and give me understanding when what I read makes little sense to me. Take my hand, Lord, as I read, and guide me on the greatest possible adventure. In Jesus' name, amen.

1. http://www.gospelpedler.com/sacredbks.html
2. http://www.wycliffe.org/wbt-usa/WBT-hist.htm
3. John Piper, *A Godward Life* (Sisters, OR: Multnomah Books, 1997), 57.

CHAPTER EIGHT

THe GReaT CoNVeRSaTIoN

Prayer is the primary way we communicate with God. Sometimes it may feel like a one-way conversation, but it really isn't. In prayer we thank God for His goodness to us, confess our sins, praise Him for who He is, and make requests of Him. Through regular times of prayer we listen for His counsel and so deepen our relationship with God and mature in our faith. Nothing is too small to bring to His attention and nothing is too big for Him to handle. We cannot grow spiritually without spending time with God in prayer—but more than that, why would we want to deny ourselves the pleasure of His company by neglecting to pray?

❝ He SAiD It ❞

All I know is that when I pray, coincidences happen and when I don't pray, they don't happen.

DAN HAYES

Some believers neglect to pray—or at least don't pray much—because they can't see the point in it. They wonder, *Why should I pray if God already knows everything?*

Here's one obvious answer to the question: we pray because God commands us to pray. "Keep on praying," He tells us (1 Thessalonians 5:17).

Since God does not give us frivolous orders, if He tells us to pray, we had better make up our minds to pray.

He SAiD It

I squirm when I see athletes praying before a game. Don't they realize that if God took sports seriously, He never would have created George Steinbrenner?

MARK RUSSELL

But consider another way to look at the question. God really does know everything, which means that the Holy Spirit, the third Person of the Trinity, also knows everything. And yet the Spirit prays for us! He does this, fully aware that the Father "knows all hearts." This fact does not deter the Spirit from praying but instead makes His prayers effective and powerful (Romans 8:26-27).

So if *God* prays when He already knows everything, then something mysterious must be happening in prayer that we don't fully understand. Therefore, if God says we should pray, we'd be wise to pray, even if we can't quite comprehend all the reasons why.

A SWeeT PaRTNeRSHiP

Consider prayer a partnership between you, others, and God (see Romans 15:30). God is calling you into action as a coworker with Him. He wants to move and act and reshape this world, not merely as a mighty outside force, but as a Senior Partner in this world collaborating with you. That's quite a compliment!

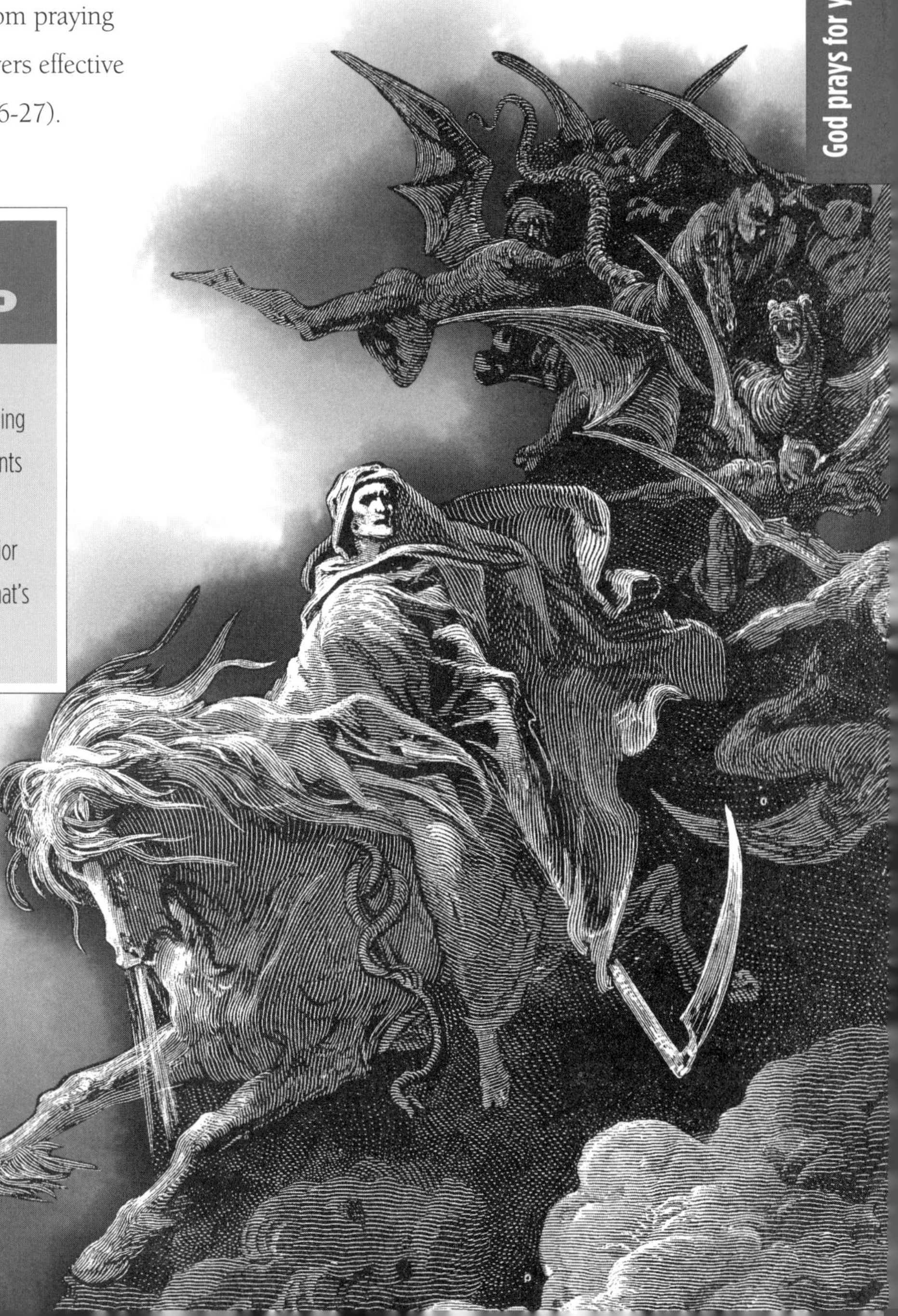

What kinds of prayer are there? That's a little like asking what kinds of conversations there are. In your own conversations, what happens? Maybe you thank a friend for a nice thing she did. Or you ask someone for help. Perhaps you remember old times, discuss a game, or just shoot the breeze. Most of the time, you don't script your conversations; they just happen in the ordinary flow of life.

Prayer is a lot like that, except you don't see the Person with whom you're speaking. Sometimes in prayer, you praise God for who He is (see Psalm 86:12) or thank Him for something He has done (see John 11:41) or ask Him for help (see Psalm 22:19). Many times, you simply talk to Him about your concerns or hopes or fears or aspirations, friend to Friend. You pour out your heart to Him and wait for His response (see Psalm 55:1-2).

He SAiD It

If you are strangers to prayer,
you are strangers to power.

BILLY SUNDAY

What should you pray about? Here's a general rule of thumb: if it concerns you, interests you, appeals to you, or frightens you, then pray about it. People in the Bible prayed about all kinds of things: for safe travel (see Ezra 8:21), for a healthy pregnancy (see 1 Samuel 1:11-13), for protection from enemies (see Nehemiah 4:9), for guidance (see Psalm 143:8), for release from prison (see Acts 12:12-17), for spiritual strength (see Ephesians 3:16), for physical health (see 3 John 1:2)—the list goes on. "Pray about everything," the Bible instructs us. "Tell God what you need, and thank him for all he has done" (Philippians 4:6).

And how should we pray? Should we kneel? Close our eyes? Speak aloud or pray silently? Pray in groups or by ourselves? Again, the Bible describes people praying in many ways. It reports silent prayer (see 1 Samuel 1:12-13), loud prayer (see Luke 23:46), extremely short prayer (see Nehemiah 2:4), long prayer (see Daniel 9:1-19), private prayer (see Matthew 6:6), public prayer (see 1 Kings 8:22-23), kneeling prayer (see Ezra 9:5-6), standing prayer (see 2 Chronicles 20:5-6)—the list goes on. Jesus probably assumed all sorts of postures when He spent whole nights in prayer (see Luke 6:12). The point is not posture, but actually praying.

Some people struggle to pray consistently because they wonder whether it does much good. Does prayer really accomplish anything?

Jesus thought so. He taught that if we pray with faith, then astonishing, and even staggering things, can take place (see Matthew 17:20). On the other hand, if we don't pray much, then we don't get much: "The reason you don't have what you want is that you don't ask God for it" (James 4:2). God refrains from doing certain things unless we first ask Him to intervene (see Matthew 7:7; John 16:24).

Does prayer accomplish anything? From the Bible's perspective, a better question would be, is there anything that prayer *can't* accomplish? Through prayer, wonders beyond our imagination occur (see Ephesians 3:20).

And why shouldn't they? After all, it isn't our prayers that do the work, but the all-powerful God to whom we pray. That's why God keeps asking us, "Is anything too hard for the LORD?" (Genesis 18:14; Jeremiah 32:27). The answer, of course, is an emphatic "No!"—because "nothing is impossible with God" (Luke 1:37).

HiGH POiNtS in HiSToRY

Alexander Maclaren (1826-1920), in his day often called "the prince of expository preachers," used the example of Abraham's testing on Mt. Moriah (see Genesis 22) to prepare his congregation for the way God often answers our prayers: "Remember, only when Abraham stands with knife in hand, expecting that the next moment it will run red with his son's blood—only then does the call come: 'Abraham!' Only then does he notice the ram caught in the thicket. That is God's way always. Up to the very edge we are driven, before He puts out His hand to help us. It is best for us that we should be brought to desperation, to say, 'My foot slips' and then, just as our toes feel the ice, help comes and His mercy holds us up. At the last moment—never before it, never until we have discovered how much we need it, and never too late—comes the Helper.[1]

An all-powerful God can do anything in response to your prayers.

But if God invites you to pray and has the power to turn your requests into reality, then why don't you always get what you pray for? Why do some of your requests seem to get turned down? Often you won't ever know the specific "why," but the Bible does suggest several possible reasons for some prayers going unanswered.

Sometimes your own sin is the culprit. Isaiah says, "Listen! The LORD is not too weak to save you, and he is not becoming deaf. He can hear you when you call. But there is a problem—your sins have cut you off from God. Because of your sin, he has turned away and will not listen anymore" (Isaiah 59:1-2; see also *James* 4:3).

Sometimes you may lack the necessary faith. When the disciples asked Jesus why they couldn't cast a demon out of a boy, He replied, "You didn't have enough faith" (Matthew 17:20; see also James 1:5-7).

Sometimes your prayers have to wait to be answered until it's God's time. This is why Jesus taught His followers "their need for constant prayer and to show them that they must never give up" (Luke 18:1).

❝ THeY SAiD It ❞

What men usually ask for when they pray to God is, that two and two may not make four.

RUSSIAN PROVERB

Mom, please pray that God would teach me patience.

Sometimes your prayers go unanswered because what you want isn't God's will for you. What you desire opposes what God desires. So John writes, "We can be confident that he will listen to us whenever we ask him for anything *in line with his will*" (1 John 5:14, emphasis added). Now, it's possible to be out of sync with God's will for a time and still not sin—otherwise, when Jesus asked His Father to spare Him from the horrors of the cross, Christ would have become a sinner Himself. You may have good dreams that still do not match God's will for you—consider King *David's* desire to build a temple in Jerusalem (see 1 Kings 8:18-19)—and yet it's no sin to dream them. God may use those unfulfilled dreams to bring you where He wants you.

Last, God may hold off on granting your request because He wants to give you something even better (see Matthew 7:9-10). Ruth Bell Graham, the wife of evangelist Billy Graham, once said, "If God had answered every prayer of mine, I would have married the wrong man seven times."

The QUeSTiON BoX

➤ What kinds of things have you been praying about?

➤ What did you say to God the last time your prayers didn't get answered as you'd hoped?

➤ Think about some of your prayers that received a "no" from God. How might His "no" have been wiser than your plea for "yes"?

The Bible suggests several reasons for unanswered prayer.

Honey, I think He Is.

We should remember at least two things about prayer: it is powerful, and it can be deeply mysterious. Give up on finding the *Three Steps to Guaranteed, Answered Prayer!* The truth is we often "don't even know what we should pray for, nor how we should pray." But God doesn't let us struggle on our own, for "the Holy Spirit prays for us with groanings that cannot be expressed in words . . . The Spirit pleads for us believers in harmony with God's own will" (Romans 8:26, 27).

Some people avoid adding the phrase "If it be Your will" to their prayers. They think it betrays a lack of faith and see it as an escape clause, as an excuse for when things turn sour or as a transparent attempt to explain why some prayers don't get answered.

But praying "If it be Your will" follows a legitimate biblical pattern (see Mark 14:36; Acts 18:21; James 4:13-16; Romans 1:10; 15:31-32). If it's wrong or foolish, then a lot of Bible heroes, including Jesus, offered either sinful or foolish prayers.

The Bible declares that we *often* don't know what to pray for. We just don't know, in many situations, what the will of God is. So should we not pray at all? No, God invites us and urges us to come to Him in prayer, especially in times of confusion (see Proverbs 2:1-5; Philippians 3:7-8; James 1:5). So we pray, make our requests known to God, and willingly submit to His will.

SeeING THe BiG PiCTuRe

A mother wanted only the best for her daughter. She often prayed that God would bring a mature Christian man into her daughter's life. One day, such a young man showed up at church—tall, handsome, a talented singer, and the daughter even seemed to catch his eye. The two were close in age, they both loved sports, and since the mother considered them a perfect match, she prayed earnestly that the two would connect. She nearly wore God out with her prayers that He make them a couple.

He didn't. In fact, they never went out on a single date—and today this mom thanks God every day for the negative answer to prayer. It turned out that the young man was not all he appeared; in fact, he had left a string of brokenhearted lovers behind, after he had stripped them of most of their money. For the longest time, no one knew anything—except God.

We see out of only one small pane of dirty glass; but God observes everything through a sparkling-clean picture window of our lives.

👀 THeY SAiD It 👀

Every man wants to pray the day before he dies.
As he does not know when his time will come,
he must pray every day in order to be safe.

JEWISH PROVERB

We all need to see God at work in our lives. We all need to know that He listens for our voices and waits to do great things for us. Jesus tells us that if we pray with even a little faith, we can partner with God to move mountains.

❝ SHE SAiD It ❞

Dear God: This is my prayer.
Could you please give my brother some brains?
So far he doesn't have any.

ANGELA, AGE 8

So how can *you* learn to pray with faith like that?

First, focus on God, not on your faith (see Mark 11:20-25). How does your trust in a friend increase? Not by locking yourself in a dark room and chanting, "I must have faith, I must have faith." No, it grows by watching your friend in all sorts of situations, by observing his or her trustworthiness in keeping secrets, in keeping promises, in keeping appointments. It's the same way with God. The more you get to know Him, the more your faith grows.

Second, review what God has done in your past (see Psalm 136). Recount what He has done in your life and in the life of your family and friends. Review past answers to prayer. Talk with others about how God has taken care of you.

Third, believe that you will have the necessary faith at the appropriate time (see Mark 13:11). At unique times and in special seasons God may give you exactly this kind of overcoming, invincible faith. But no one in the Bible—not even Jesus—always prayed with this sort of mountain-moving faith. The Bible says that even faith is a gift of God (see Romans 12:3; 1 Corinthians 12:9), and the Lord distributes His gifts when and where He chooses (see 1 Corinthians 12:11).

Still, if He can make a donkey speak with the voice of a human (see Numbers 22:28), then He can give you the necessary faith at the appropriate time—so long as you have been *walk*ing faithfully with Him all along.

THe DiFFeReNCe BeTWeeN DouBT and QUeSTIONS

Having questions is not the same as harboring doubt! Doubt says, "It can't be," "It's not possible," "No, I'm not worthy." Questions say, "How will this be?" "I don't understand," "May it be according to your Word." To see the big difference, compare Luke 1:11-20 with Luke 1:26-38.

For the most part, it feels wonderful to communicate with God in prayer. To be able to freely bring to Him your fears, your hopes, your joys, your sorrows, and then to listen and watch for His response—could anything beat connecting with the God of the universe on a personal, spirit-to-Spirit level?

Remember, though, that prayer is essentially communication with God, similar on many levels to your communication with others. So ask yourself a question: is *all* your communication with

others fun? Probably not. Sometimes you have to talk about unpleasant or dark things—when you've hurt someone or he's hurt you, when you've messed up, when you can sense a growing distance in your relationship. If you want to heal the wounds and get back on the right track, then you have to set your communications dial to the "REPAIR" mode.

The same thing is true in your walk of faith. It's a necessary part of growing in your relationship with God.

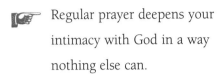

So What?

☞ Regular prayer deepens your intimacy with God in a way nothing else can.

☞ God gives you many of His best gifts only in response to prayer.

☞ Through prayer, God gives you insight and guidance that you wouldn't have otherwise.

❝ SHe SAiD It ❞

Dear God:
I didn't think orange went with purple until
I saw the sunset you made on Tuesday.

MARGARET

SHeEP TaLK

Dear Lord, it's amazing that You invite me to come into Your presence, anytime of day or night, and pour out my heart to You. It amazes me that You not only listen to my prayers, but that You respond to them in power, both for Your glory and my benefit. Help me to listen for Your voice, Lord, and to watch for Your answers. I know You have a flair for the surprising and the dramatic! Most of all, Lord, prompt me to keep connected to You through prayer because I love spending time with You. In Jesus' name, amen.

1. Steve Halliday, *Faith Is Stranger Then Fiction* (Green Forest, AR: New Leaf Press, 2000), 144.

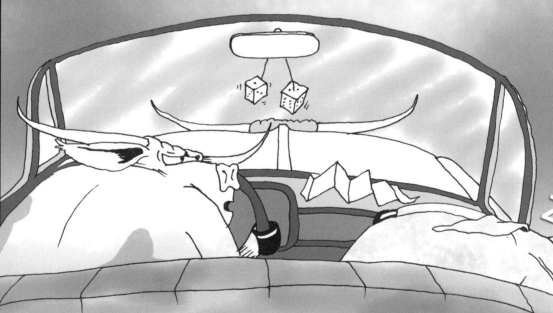

CHAPTER NINE

WHeN THiNGS Go BaD

Have you ever watched a toddler learn to walk? Eager adults crowd around, encouraging the little one to take those first few steps. They reach out their hands, inviting the child to move in their direction. And then it happens! One little foot steps unsteadily in front of the other, and with smiles and applause breaking out all around, another little human makes its wobbly entrance into the world of walking.

And yet, things don't always go right. Sometimes, one foot lands on the other and the toddler comes crashing down. Or he puts too much weight forward and comes crashing down. Or she just gets tired and comes crashing down. Every toddler soon learns that failure is part of the process of learning to walk.

It's not much different in a walk of faith. Things don't always go right. We screw up, sometimes unintentionally and sometimes on purpose, and come crashing down. The question then becomes, how do we get back up and start walking again?

❝ He SAiD It ❞

Mistakes are a part of being human. Appreciate your mistakes for what they are: precious life lessons that can be learned only the hard way. Unless it's a fatal mistake, which, at least, others can learn from.

AL FRANKEN

When we take a misstep in our walk of faith—whether we do something to offend God or someone else—the first order of business comes down to one word: repentance. To get back on the right track, we have to "repent" of what we did.

And what is repentance? The most common Old Testament word for "repentance" means "a radical change in one's attitude toward sin and God. The term implies a . . . personal decision to forsake sin and enter into fellowship with God."[1] The most common word in the New Testament refers to "a complete change of one's way of life . . . change of mind is the dominant idea . . . while the accompanying grief and reform of life are necessary consequences."[2]

He SAiD It

Admitting Error clears the Score
And proves you Wiser than before.

ARTHUR GUITERMAN

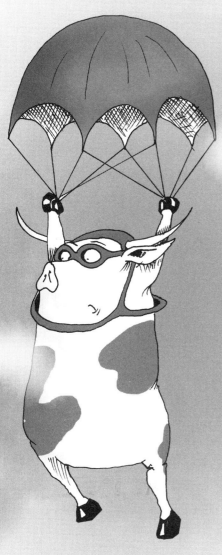

To repent is to abandon your sin and pursue God.

To repent means to recognize that we have done wrong, to grieve over what we have done, and to consciously choose to stop doing the wrong thing and start doing the right thing. We change our minds about our behavior and so change the direction we were walking.

John the Baptist, the cousin of Jesus, cut to the chase when he told the crowds following him, "Turn from your sins and turn to God" (Matthew 3:2).

Peter said the same thing to the people of Jerusalem: "Now turn from your sins and turn to God, so you can be cleansed of your sins" (Acts 3:19). So did Paul: "All must turn from their sins and turn to God—and prove they have changed by the good things they do" (Acts 26:20).[3] We cannot move ahead in our walk of faith if we refuse to turn around when we're heading in the wrong direction.

Who needs to repent? Whoever takes a wrong spiritual turn, whoever does wrong—in the Bible's terms, whoever sins. Peter declared, "Each of you must turn from your sins and turn to God" (Acts 2:38). God "does not want anyone to perish, so he is giving more time for everyone to repent" (2 Peter 3:9).

Do you ever take a wrong spiritual turn? Do you ever do wrong? Do you ever sin? Of course you do. We *all* do. So that means you have to learn and practice the drill of repentance.

WHaT NoW?

Since we all sin, we all need to repent. But we might try a few things to keep us from having to repent so often, according to one unknown writer: "What settings are you in when you fall? Avoid them. What props do you have that support your sin? Eliminate them. What people are you usually with? Avoid them. There are two equally damning lies Satan wants us to believe:

1) Just once won't hurt

2) Now that you have ruined your life, you are beyond God's use, and might as well enjoy sinning."

REPENT! END IS NEAR!

How often do you need to repent? As often as you sin. Paul had to write to some unrepentant Christian friends, "I am afraid that when I come, God will humble me again because of you. And I will have to grieve because many of you who sinned earlier have not repented of your impurity, sexual immorality, and eagerness for lustful pleasure" (2 Corinthians 12:21). These believers had sinned but had not repented of it. And Paul couldn't allow them to continue walking such a destructive path unchallenged.

As soon as we realize we have stepped off of God's good path for us, we need to repent. We need to change our minds about our spiritual direction, turn around, and start walking God's way once more.

SHe SAiD It

If you have made mistakes, even serious ones, there is always another chance for you. What we call failure is not the falling down but the staying down.

MARY PICKFORD

As soon as you realize you're going in the wrong spiritual direction, turn around and start going the right way.

True repentance always leads to genuine confession. God tells us to confess our sins, to name them and admit them, out loud.

Why should we have to confess our sins? Why not just repent silently, change our behavior by tapping into the power of the Holy Spirit, and leave it at that? What's the point of confession?

Much of the power of sin lies in its being kept secret. It gets stronger the longer you allow it to hide in the dark. Confession breaks the power that sin gains over you. King David wrote, "When I refused to confess my sin, I was weak and miserable, and I groaned all day long. Day and night your hand of discipline was heavy on me. My strength evaporated like water in the summer heat. Finally, I confessed all my sins to you and stopped trying to hide them. I said to myself, 'I will confess my rebellion to the LORD.' And you forgave me! All my guilt is gone" (Psalm 32:3-5).

❝ He SAiD It ❞

Forgiveness is always free. But that doesn't mean that confession is always easy. Sometimes it is hard. Incredibly hard. It is painful to admit our sins and entrust ourselves to God's care.

ERWIN W. LUTZER

All the godly people of the Bible—with the exception of Jesus, who never once sinned [4]—had to learn how to confess their sins in order to keep moving ahead in their walk of faith. Bible heroes like David the king (see 2 Samuel 12:13), Daniel the wise man (see Daniel 9:5), Micah the prophet (see Micah 7:9), Paul the apostle (see 1 Timothy 1:16) and all the rest saw confession as a necessary part of their spiritual journey. Throughout the Bible, we see confession repeatedly commanded and illustrated. [5]

The QUeSTiON BoX

➤ Think through your week. Is any sin lurking around that you have not confessed? If so, name it, out loud.

➤ Tell God you're sorry for what you did or said or thought. Ask Him to help you change your mind about the sin and start walking His way again.

➤ Was another person involved? If so, how can you best go to him or her and ask for forgiveness?

➤ When God forgives, He forgives completely; He thinks about it no longer. Neither should you.

When you confess your sins you break their power over you.

SHEEP/WOLF
WOLF/SHEEP
DICTIONARY

Yee-HAW!

Four people shared a berth in a train going from Paris to Madrid: a beautiful young woman, her grandmother, a handsome young army lieutenant, and the man's commanding officer.

When the train passed through a tunnel, everything became pitch-black. Without warning there came the sound of a kiss, followed by a slap. When the train emerged from the tunnel, the four sat stone-faced, as if nothing had happened.

The beautiful young woman thought, *That was a wonderful kiss, but my grandmother must have slapped his face and he probably thinks I did it and he won't pay attention to me again.*

The grandmother thought, *That's a fresh thing for that man to kiss my granddaughter. I'm sure glad she stood up for herself; I'm sure it will teach him a lesson.*

The commanding officer thought, *This is terrible, she must have thought that I was the one who kissed her. Wait until I get back to the base! I'm really going to give my lieutenant a piece of my mind.*

And the handsome young lieutenant thought, *This was my day. I got to kiss a beautiful woman and slap my boss—and get away with both!*

So to whom are you supposed to confess your sins? First, of course, God tells you to confess your wrongdoings to Him.

The apostle John writes, "If we confess our sins to him, he is faithful and just to forgive us and to cleanse us from every wrong" (1 John 1:9). Even after you place your faith in Christ and God washes your spiritual slate completely clean and makes you fit for heaven, you still need to confess your sins. Why? Not only because hidden or covered up sins gain great power over you, but because your relationship with God is a real one. You confess your sins to God when you screw up for the same reason that you profess your love for Him when you worship. You wouldn't want to say, "God, I told You I loved You when I first came to faith, so don't expect to hear it anymore," would you? Hardly. A real relationship takes real work to maintain and grow. And part of that work is admitting the ugly truth when you screw up.

He SAiD It

Why do people not confess vices? It is because they have not yet laid them aside. It is a waking person only who can tell his dreams.

SENECA

Because a growing Christian faith is all about building healthy relationships, God also instructs us to confess our sins to each other. "Confess your sins to each other and pray for each other so that you may be healed," the Bible says (James 5:16). This doesn't mean, of course, that you blab your errors to everyone you meet. Sadly, some believers cannot be trusted with such sensitive information; they'll use it to start rumors and hurt you and your reputation. So be careful about to whom you confess your sins. Make sure it's a trustworthy friend, a maturing believer who will use the information to help you grow in faith and get back on track. And remember this: because we all sin, someday you may be able to return the favor.

Help!

Always confess your sins to God; when appropriate, confess them to mature Christian friends.

By repenting of our sins and confessing them, we reestablish the kind of healthy communication and positive personal interaction that builds strong relationships. Genuine confession opens the door to *forgiveness* and restoration.

ONLiNe FoRGiVeNeSS?

Is it possible to give and receive forgiveness online? Anonymously? Without any intentional contact between the offended and the offender? Just type in "forgiveness" on your web browser, and you're likely to see a host of websites dedicated to discussing, highlighting, pondering, and studying the topic of forgiveness. At least one site has an "Apology Room" that provides guests the opportunity to "anonymously share with others those things for which you are sorry." These sites raise a few questions:

➤ Is feeling "truly sorry" the same as seeking forgiveness?

➤ Is saying "I apologize" the same as saying "Will you forgive me"?

➤ Is claiming "I never meant to hurt you" the same as asking for forgiveness?

💬 He SAiD It 💬

The glory of Christianity is to conquer by forgiveness.

WILLIAM BLAKE

That means that once you've repented of some sin and confessed it to God, you don't have to keep beating yourself up over it. Some Christians seldom feel any joy in their relationship with Jesus because they're just *sure* that they live under the perpetual frown of God. They never feel good enough, holy enough, successful enough.

But remind yourself of what God says about those who repent, confess, and trust Him for forgiveness. "He has removed our rebellious acts as far away from us as the east is from the west" the psalmist exclaims (Psalm 103:12). "You will trample our sins under your feet and throw them into the depths of the ocean!" exults the prophet Micah (Micah 7:19).

Perhaps James put it as well as anyone: "Draw close to God, and God will draw close to you" (James 4:8). You can bank on it!

❝ He SAiD It ❞

If I owe Smith ten dollars and God
forgives me, that doesn't pay Smith.

ROBERT GREEN INGERSOLL

Once you and God have gotten back on the same page, you may need to get busy on some relationship repairs with others. Sin has a nasty way of not only hurting our day-to-day relationship with God but also damaging our relationships with family members, friends, and others. So God tells us, "You must make allowance for each other's faults and forgive the person who offends you. Remember, the Lord forgave you, so you must forgive others" (Colossians 3:13; see also Matthew 18:21-35).

👀 He SAiD It 👀

He that cannot forgive others, breaks the
bridge over which he himself must pass
if he would ever reach heaven.

GEORGE HERBERT

At times, you're the one who needs to forgive someone who hurt you. You may not feel like it; you may not want to; it may seem as if you're letting the person "off the hook." But God says that forgiving others is a big part of what He expects His children to do.

"If you forgive those who sin against you, your heavenly Father will forgive you," Jesus said. "But if you refuse to forgive others, your Father will not forgive your sins" (Matthew 6:14-15). It's *that* important.

At other times, you're the one who needs to seek and receive the forgiveness of someone you have hurt. For many of us, this can be a much harder job. Maybe your behavior still embarrasses you, or you don't feel worthy of receiving forgiveness, or you think you first have to pay your dues. While the Bible certainly instructs us to make restitution whenever possible,[6] it doesn't insist that we do five years of hard penance before we can receive the forgiveness of someone who offers it. Instead, God's Word counsels us, "Be kind to each other, tenderhearted, forgiving one another, just as God through Christ has forgiven you" (Ephesians 4:32).

A walk of faith doesn't always go smoothly. We all encounter problems along the way, some caused by others, some that we cause, and some from sources unknown. Conflicts erupt.

Disagreements occur. Hurt feelings multiply. But God wants to use even these struggles to shape us into people who more closely resemble His Son.

In fact, God allows and even designs many of these problems to test the reality of our faith. We say we believe—but how do we react when troubles come? During such testing times, we reveal what we really believe about a life of faith.

So What?

☞ Genuine repentance clears away the relationship rubble that prevents you from enjoying a vibrant connection with your heavenly Father.

☞ Genuine repentance breaks the power that secret sins gain over you.

☞ Genuine repentance leads to forgiveness and the restoration of damaged relationships.

❝❝ He SAiD It ❝❝

Unless we know the difference between flowers and weeds, we are not fit to take care of a garden. It is not enough to have truth planted in our minds. We must learn and labor to keep the ground clear of thorns and briars, follies and perversities, which have a wicked propensity to choke the word of life.

CLYDE FRANCIS LYTLE

SHeEP TaLK

Lord, You tell us in the Bible that we all stumble in many ways—and I *know* that's true in my case. Please help me, not only to recognize when I stumble, but also to do what I can to make things right with anyone I have offended or hurt. Build into me the good habits of repentance, confession, and forgiveness, so that I will never let things ride for too long before I turn around and once more start walking on the right path and in the right direction. In Jesus' name, amen.

1. G.W. Bromiley, ed., *The International Standard Bible Encyclopedia*, Fully Revised, Vol 4 (Grand Rapids, MI: William B. Eerdmans Publishing Co., 1988), 135.
2. Ibid, 136.
3. See also 2 Chronicles 6:36-39; Ezekiel 18:30-32; Acts 20:21; Romans 2:4-5; 2 Corinthians 7:8-11; 2 Timothy 2:23-26; Revelation 2:4-5, 14-16; 3:1-3, 15-20.
4. See also Leviticus 5:5; Numbers 5:5-7; 1 Samuel 7:5-6; Ezra 10:1-12; Nehemiah 9:1-3; Acts 19:18-19.
5. See also Matthew 5:23-24; Mark 11:25; Luke 17:3-5; 2 Corinthians 2:5-11.
6. See, for example, Exodus 22:1; Proverbs 14:9; Luke 19:8.

CHAPTER TEN

SeTTLeR, TouRiST, oR PiLGRim?

Do you think in pictures? Probably so; most of us do, and we almost can't help it. We seem wired to speak and imagine in concrete images, using mental pictures of familiar objects. Even people considered abstract thinkers usually rely on pictures more than you might expect.

Albert Einstein, for example—the genius who gave us the highly abstract concepts of special and general relativity, as well as that most famous of equations, $E = MC^2$—began most of his scientific explorations with what he called "thought experiments." Before he worked out the complex mathematics of special relativity,

he first imagined what it would feel like to ride a lightning bolt through the universe.

Mental images have great power. How you picture a thing can have tremendous implications for how you live. And that's true for a life of faith, too.

😮 He SAiD It 😮

You see, wire telegraph is a kind of a very, very long cat. You pull his tail in New York and his head is meowing in Los Angeles. Do you understand this? And radio operates exactly the same way: you send signals here, they receive them there. The only difference is that there is no cat.

ALBERT EINSTEIN

Author Wes Seeliger understands the power of images. Many years ago he wrote a hilarious and provocative picture book titled *Western Theology*. He thought that many believers had settled for a closed life without adventure, largely because of how they pictured their faith. He used the image of a settler (in contrast to a pioneer) to describe their experience: "Fear of all change, the desire to 'protect' God, the return to Old Time Religion (i.e., 19th Century revivalism), religion as a retreat from a dangerous world, and so on."[1] For believers like these, a life of faith is safe, predictable, highly controlled, and . . . well, *boring*.

SHe SAiD It

Security is mostly a superstition. It does not exist in nature, nor do the children of men as a whole experience it. Avoiding danger is no safer in the long run than outright exposure. Life is either a daring adventure or nothing.

HELEN KELLER

SETTLER CITY

Settle down.
Keep your voice low.
Keep your nose clean.

THE HONORABLE
ALPHA O. MEGA
Mayor

In Settler Theology, the church is a dusty old courthouse; God is a distant and rarely seen mayor ("THE HONOR-ABLE ALPHA O. MEGA"); Jesus is a sheriff who makes sure people uphold the law; the Holy Spirit is a saloon girl, Miss Dove, who keeps the settlers happy; and the pastor is a bank teller.

Christians live in Settler City, waiting for the Last Roundup when they

GoNe FoR GooD

Visitors to a deserted shack near Chadron, Nebraska, have taken note of the sad but firm message carved on the building's sagging timbers:

30 miles to water, 20 miles to wood,
10 miles to hell and I gone there for good.

expect to join the Settlers Triumphant at that Great Golden Ranch in the sky. Their goal is to keep in good with the mayor and stay out of the sheriff's way. "The town may be dull," Seeliger says, "but it's not dangerous. Unless the Mayor calls him prematurely, a Settler is pretty likely to live his three score and ten and die in bed an undisturbed man."[2]

Those who picture their faith as would a Settler miss the whole point of the Christian life. God does not call you to settle down and get comfortable, to keep your voice low and your nose clean while you wait for heaven. And if you think He does, then read 2 Corinthians 11:20-29 sometime.

QueSTIoNS TouRiSTS ASK

Park rangers around the country have been asked some pretty... er... amazing questions by addled tourists. Among them:

Grand Canyon National Park

- Was this man-made?
- Do you light it up at night?
- Where are the faces of the presidents?

Denali National Park

- Can you show me where the Yeti lives?
- How often do you mow the tundra?
- How much does Mount McKinley weigh?

Mesa Verde National Park

- Did people build this, or did Indians?
- Why did they build the ruins so close to the road?
- Do you know of any undiscovered ruins?

Carlsbad Caverns National Park

- How much of the cave is underground?
- So what's in the unexplored part of the cave?
- So what is this—just a hole in the ground?

Yellowstone National Park

- Does Old Faithful erupt at night?
- How do you turn it on?
- We had no trouble finding the park entrances, but where are the exits?

Other believers have a different, but equally faulty, picture in mind of the Christian life. They don't want to settle down and get comfortable so much as they want to travel around and get entertained. They don't buy into Settler Theology, but they do get excited about Tourist Theology.

Believers who think of themselves as Tourists observe the bustle of the world around them without really touching it. They may like to take snapshots of where they've been, but they don't want to sample the food, mix with the people, appreciate the culture, or get involved in any way. They're just as happy to snap their pictures from inside the window of their tour bus as they are to actually step outside. They like to be entertained and have a good time—and getting involved in real life can ruin everything.

He SAiD It

The world does not need tourists who ride by in a bus clucking their tongues. The world as it is needs those who will love it enough to change it, with what they have, where they are.

ROBERT FULGHUM

Tourist Christians might actually have some sympathy for the fabricated quote attributed a few years ago to a pop princess: "When I watch TV and see those poor, starving kids all over the world, I can't help but cry. I mean, I'd love to be skinny like that, but not with all those flies and death and stuff."

Christians who see themselves as Tourists want to feel a part of the action without really getting in on it, and if the trip isn't all they'd expected, they demand a refund. They crave all of the excitement of life with none of the risk. And they have an impossible time trying to identify with believers like **Barnabas** and Paul, who "risked their lives for the sake of our Lord Jesus Christ" (Acts 15:26). Risking anything for their faith just doesn't make sense to them.

Reject a "Tourist" mind-set—hands-off, entertainment-focused, and risk-free.

If you want to grow as a Christian, you can't live your life according to either Settler Theology or Tourist Theology. Instead, the Bible points you toward a different approach, something that might be called Pilgrim Theology.

Now, when you think *Pilgrim*, don't imagine tall hats, big buckles, wardrobes mostly of black, and picnic tables full of turkey and pumpkins

He SAiD It

The only ultimate disaster that can befall us, I have come to realize, is to feel ourselves at home here on earth.

MALCOLM MUGGERIDGE

surrounded by happy native Americans and weary Europeans fresh off the *Mayflower*. Think instead of **Abraham**.

In many ways, Abraham is our chief example for a life of faith. He lived thousands of years before Christ and centuries before Moses, but the Bible says of him, "Abraham is the spiritual father of those who have faith . . . Abraham is the father of all who believe" (Romans 4:11, 16).

How was Abraham a Pilgrim? Abraham lived by faith, which meant that when God told him to leave his home and go someplace else, "he went without knowing where he was going." Even when Abraham reached the *Promised Land*, "he was like a foreigner, living in a tent." Abraham and his descendants "agreed that they were no more than foreigners and nomads here on earth." That is, they were Pilgrims, wayfarers, people who journey in foreign lands (Hebrews 11:8-9).

And why did Abraham live like this? He did so "because he was confidently looking forward to a city with eternal foundations, a city designed and built by God." He and

The QUeSTiON BoX

Imagine that God sends you on a trip, to a place you've never been, to do something you've never done.

➤ What do you want to take with you? Why?

➤ Whom do you want take with you? Why?

➤ How are you going to get there? And once you arrive—what then?

his descendants were "looking forward to a country they can call their own," not the land they had left behind, but "a better place, a heavenly homeland" (Hebrews 11:10, 14, 16). Abraham thought of himself as "a stranger in a foreign land" (Genesis 23:4).[3]

And that's exactly the right mental picture for anyone who wants to succeed in the Christian life.

The early disciples understood the importance of thinking of themselves as pilgrims. Peter reminded some Christian friends, "Dear brothers and sisters, you are foreigners and aliens here. So I warn you to keep away from evil desires because they fight against your very souls" (1 Peter 2:11). Paul described some foolish people whose "god is their appetite, they brag about shameful things, and all they think about is this life here on earth." In contrast, Paul declared, "we are citizens of heaven, where the Lord Jesus Christ lives. And we are eagerly waiting for him to return as our Savior" (Philippians 3:19, 20).

He SAiD It

In God's country there are no barriers, no walls or curtains to divide; no race barrier; no soldiers because there are no wars; no policemen because there is no crime or sin; no undertakers because there are no graves; no physicians because germs, fevers, pestilences, diseases are unknown; no thieves because there is no darkness. Who would not yearn for this better and more desirable country in which there are no separations, no broken homes, no drunkards, no prisons, no hospitals, no beggars, no persons who are blind, deaf, dumb or destitute? What a country! Are you not homesick for Heaven?

HERBERT LOCKYER

WooDY's TaKe

Comedian Woody Allen thinks a lot about death and life (and maybe in that order).
What do you think of his take on the subjects?

➤ "I don't want to achieve immortality through my work. I want to achieve it through not dying."

➤ "I'm not afraid to die. I just don't want to be there when it happens."

➤ "Life is full of misery, loneliness, and suffering—and it's all over much too soon."

Only a Pilgrim Christian can experience life fully, as God intended. Such a person fully engages with the adventure of living, yet holds all of life with an open hand, so he can honestly say, "For to me, living is for Christ, and dying is even better" (Philippians 1:21). She lives positively with a strong future orientation and so says things like, "We are looking forward to the new heavens and new earth he has promised, a world where everyone is right with God" (2 Peter 3:13). And he or she understands that God will honor *all* of His promises, even if He takes until the next life to do it.

He SAiD It

I think that there were only two people in my high school that were comfortable there, and I think they are both pumping gas now.

GRANT SHOW, ACTOR

Engage fully with the adventure of living, yet hold all of life with an open hand.

Bestselling author C. S. Lewis also grasped the importance of living a Pilgrim lifestyle. In a letter to a friend he once wrote, "All joy . . . emphasizes our pilgrim status; always reminds, beckons, awakens desire. Our best havings are wantings."[4]

Nothing on earth can ultimately satisfy our hearts, but God can fill those same hearts to overflowing. That's why the psalmist could cry out joyfully to God, "Whom have I in heaven but you? I desire you more than anything on earth" (Psalm 73:25).

But does such a heavenly outlook make a person useless on earth? Hardly. In his classic book *Mere Christianity*, Lewis wrote, "If you read history you will find that the Christians who did most for the present world were just those who thought most of the next . . . It is since Christians have largely ceased to think of the other world that they have become so ineffective in this. Aim at Heaven and you will get earth 'thrown in': aim at earth and you will get neither."[5]

Pilgrim believers throughout the centuries have crossed oceans, defied kings, walked into war zones, assisted the sick, built schools, delivered food, helped prisoners, and risked (and often lost) their lives precisely because they believed God when He said, "Since everything around us is going to melt away, what holy, godly lives you should be living! You should look forward to that day and hurry it along" (2 Peter 3:11-12).

He SAiD It

He whose head is in heaven need not fear to put his feet into the grave.

MATTHEW HENRY

Yee-HAW!

Two old men had been best friends for years. When one of them became terminally ill, the other visited him on his deathbed. After reminiscing for some time, the healthy man said to his friend, "Listen, Al. When you die, do me a favor, will you? I want to know if there's baseball in heaven."

The dying man readily agreed and said, "Bill, we've been friends for years. Sure, I'll do it." A short while later Al died.

A few days after the funeral, a sleeping Bill heard his deceased buddy's voice. "I've got some good news and some bad news," Al said. "The good news is that there's baseball in heaven."

"Great!" replied Bill. "What's the bad news?"

"The bad news is that you're pitching on Wednesday."

A "Pilgrim" mind-set makes you more effective in this world, not less.

Be honest: Do you think of yourself as a Settler? As a Tourist? Or as a Pilgrim? What picture comes to mind when you ponder the Christian life? And how are the pictures in your head influencing the way you live?

So What?

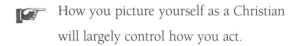

☞ How you picture yourself as a Christian will largely control how you act.

☞ Only by holding all of life with a grateful, open hand can you engage fully with the grand adventure of living.

☞ Considering yourself as a stranger in a foreign land will bring you more joy and effectiveness, not less.

He SAiD It

A ship in a harbor is safe,
but that is not what ships are built for.

WILLIAM SHEDD

SHeEP TaLK

Lord, teach me how to effectively backpack through life. Guide me as I get deeply involved in the hurting lives around me and as I help out however I can. Let Your amazing promise of heaven shape how I live on earth, but don't allow me to get so heavenly minded that I become no earthly good. And never let me get so comfortable with my current surroundings that I forget why You put me here! Teach me from the life of Abraham and mold me into a person of genuine faith. In Jesus' name, amen.

---

1 Wes Seeliger, *Western Theology* (Atlanta: Forum House, 1973), 13.

2 Ibid., 92.

3 You'll find the best picture of Abraham as a pilgrim in Hebrews 11:8-16, the passage from which these quotes are taken. Read the whole passage and try to see how your own life compares.

4 http://www.comnett.net/~rex/cslewis.htm

5 C.S. Lewis, *Mere Christianity* (New York: Macmillan Publishing Company, 1952), 118.

CHAPTER ELEVEN

THE RAPTURE...
a one-way,
all-expense-paid
trip for all
eternity...
NO BAGGAGE ALLOWED.

KEEP
LOOKING UP...
GOD IS LOOKING
DOWN.

RAPTURE
...separation of
Church & State.

PeRHaPS ToDaY!

God wants you to focus on the practical aspects of Christ's return.

With growing turmoil in the Middle East and with millions of readers devouring books about prophecy, people are thinking about the *Second Coming* of Christ more today than they have in many years. Unfortunately, much of that attention gets focused on *timing:* when is Jesus coming back?

The New Testament conspicuously lacks such a focus. Instead, it repeatedly emphasizes the practical implications of Jesus' return. Since He may come at any time, the Bible tells us, we need to be ready—and in the meantime, God wants us to use all our resources so that we "will make the teaching about God our Savior attractive in every way" (Titus 2:10).

❝ He SAiD It ❞

From time to time, as we all know, a sect appears in our midst announcing that the world will very soon come to an end. Generally, by some slight confusion or miscalculation, it is the sect that comes to an end.

G. K. CHESTERTON

Did you know that the return of Jesus Christ is the second most common doctrine in the Bible? The Bible mentions it or alludes to it some 329 times—almost three times more references than to His first coming![1] Don't ever minimize the importance of the Second Coming. The Bible would never mention it so often if it were merely some quirky doctrine on the outskirts of Christian teaching.

TOP BIBLE THEMES

1

2 Second Coming of Christ

3

4

Survey says...

He SAiD It

If our hopes, whatever we protest, really lie in this world instead of in the eternal order, we shall find it difficult to accept the New Testament teaching of the Second Coming. In our eyes, the job is not yet done; and such an action would be, though we would not put it so, an interference. But suppose our hope rests in the purpose of God: then we safely leave the timing of the earthly experiment to Him. Meanwhile, we do what we were told to do—to be alert and to work and pray for the spread of His Kingdom.

J.B. PHILLIPS

A host of biblical writers spoke of the Second Coming—and we're not talking "second stringers"! Consider just a few of the heavyweights who repeatedly draw our attention to Jesus' return:

➤ Jesus Himself (see John 14:3)

➤ An angel (see Acts 1:11)

➤ The apostle Paul
   (see 1 Thessalonians 4:16)

➤ Enoch (see Jude 1:14)

➤ The writer to the Hebrews
   (see Hebrews 10:37)

➤ The apostle Peter (see 1 Peter 5:4)

➤ The apostle John (see Revelation 1:7)

All of these messengers of God tell us that Jesus Christ—the one born in Bethlehem, the one who died on a cross and rose from the dead so that we might live with Him forever—is most certainly coming back to earth again.

A GoOD QUeSTIoN

What will you do with Jesus?
Neutral you cannot be.
One day your heart will be asking,
"What will He do with me?"

C.S. LEWIS

So when is Jesus returning? When can we expect to see Him again? No one but God knows the answer to that question—and no "secret messages" in the Bible wait to be decoded to reveal the date to you, contrary to what some claim.

Before His crucifixion, Jesus told us emphatically, "No one knows the day or the hour when these things will happen, not even the angels in heaven or the Son himself. Only the Father knows" (Matthew 24:36). After His resurrection and just moments before He returned to heaven, His disciples asked Him again, "Lord, are you going to free Israel now and restore our kingdom?" You can almost hear Him sigh as He replies, "The Father sets those dates, and they are not for you to know" (Acts 1:6, 7).

When will Jesus come again? *Nobody* knows, and don't let anyone tell you that he does. How could God make it any clearer?

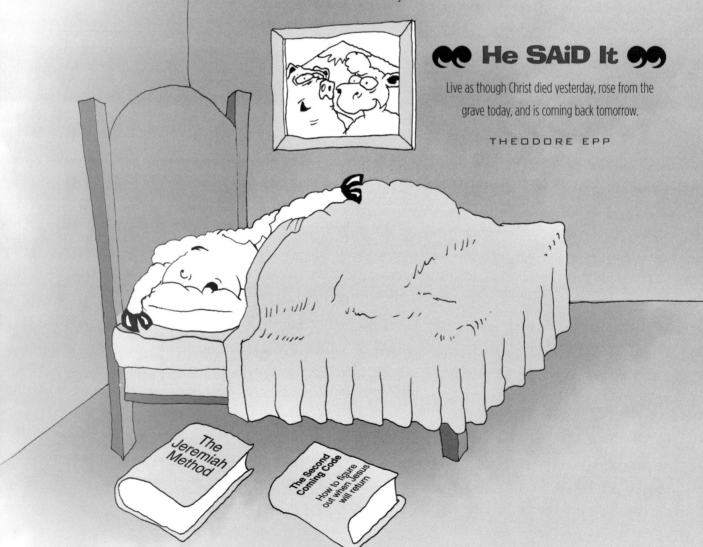

He SAiD It

Live as though Christ died yesterday, rose from the grave today, and is coming back tomorrow.

THEODORE EPP

The Jeremiah Method

The Second Coming Code
How to figure out when Jesus will return

What if God meant, quite literally, that Jesus could return at *any* moment? What if He wanted us to spend our time living for Him so that others would be attracted to the gospel, rather than spending our time trying to figure out precisely *when*? Then maybe He'd say something like this:

"So be prepared, because you don't know what day your Lord is coming. Know this: A homeowner who knew exactly when a burglar was coming would stay alert and not permit the house to be broken into. You also must be ready all the time. For the Son of Man will come when least expected" (Matthew 24:42-44; see also Luke 12:40; 1 Thessalonians 5:2).

STRiKe THaT DaTe

Despite Jesus' clear statements that nobody knows when He will return, plenty of people throughout history have insisted that they had uncovered the timetable for the Second Coming. Consider a few recent, less-than-accurate predictions.

- Edgar Whisenant sold 4.5 million copies of a book called *88 Reasons Why the Rapture Will Be in 1988!* When the Lord failed to return as advertised, Whisenant redid his figures and realized he had left out the year 0 in his calculations. A sequel, *Final Shout*, predicted the Lord would return in 1989 (it sold far fewer copies).

- Lee Jang Rim, a Korean pastor, taught that the Rapture would occur on October 28, 1992, at 10:00 a.m. EST. When it didn't happen, many of his followers allegedly committed suicide.

- David Koresh, leader of the Branch Davidian cult, calculated that the end would occur in 1995. After a 51-day standoff with law enforcement officials in Waco, Texas, 76 cult members died on April 10, 1993, as a result of a fire deliberately set by cult leaders.

- Onetime building-contractor-turned-Christian-radio-broadcaster Harold Camping predicted the Lord would return in September of 1994. As the date approached, Camping said he might have miscalculated and Jesus could return as late as October 2, 1994.

- The Vortex of the Star of David sect of Luskville, Quebec, Canada, predicted the end of the world would come on March 8, 1997.

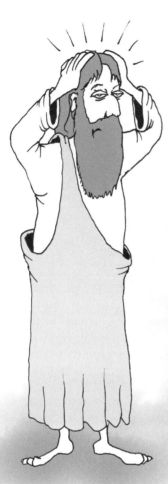

God never meant for the Bible's prophecies about Jesus' Second Coming to fuel heated debate about the timing of His Son's return. Instead, He meant them to serve some very practical purposes in our day-to-day lives. In fact, the Bible connects the truth about Jesus' return to almost every aspect of our experience.

He DeFiNiTeLY SAiD It

Don't let anyone mislead you. For many will come in my name, claiming to be the Messiah and saying, "The time has come!" But don't believe them.

JESUS CHRIST
IN LUKE 21:8

What about our life in the church? In fact, the Bible connects the Second Coming to several things we usually associate with "church stuff," such as:

➤ The Lord's Supper (1 Corinthians 11:26; Matthew 26:28-29).

➤ Ministry to others (2 Timothy 4:1-2).

➤ Pastoral roles (1 Peter 5:1-4).

➤ Funerals (1 Thessalonians 4:13-14).

➤ Congregational worship (Hebrews 12:28).

In every one of these cases, the reminder that Jesus is coming back—*perhaps today!*—is intended to profoundly influence what we do and how we behave in church. But don't get the idea that Christ's return is meant to impact church activities alone!

The reality of the Second Coming is to have a profound effect on your church life.

FIRE! PESTILENCE! WAR! and other neat stuff soon to afflict your pagan neighbors

MID

1984

The QUeSTiON BoX

1. In an average week, how often do you think about Jesus' return to earth?

2. What thoughts come to mind when you ponder the Second Coming?

3. If Jesus were to come back today, would you be ready? Explain.

If we genuinely understood the Bible's teaching about the Second Coming, it would markedly change the spiritual climate in our homes. If we took seriously what happens when Jesus comes back, including the part about divine judgment, we'd live very differently from how most polls and surveys tell us that we actually do.

❝ He SAiD It ❞

The future has a way of arriving unannounced.

GEORGE WILL

For one thing, we'd take our marriage vows a lot more seriously: "Give honor to marriage, and remain faithful to one another in marriage. God will surely judge people who are immoral and those who commit adultery" (Hebrews 13:4). This isn't a possibility or a perhaps; it's a certainty.

For another thing, we'd get a lot more serious about our prayer lives. Peter says, "The end of the world is coming soon. Therefore, be earnest and disciplined in your prayers"

(1 Peter 4:7). If you knew that Jesus was coming back in a week, do you think you'd get busy about praying for your loved ones who don't yet know Him?

Yee-HAW!

"We will all die someday," said a Bible study leader to the members of his group, "and none of us knows when. But if we did, we would all do a better job of preparing ourselves. So what would you do if you knew you had only four weeks of life left before Judgment Day?"

One man said, "I would go out into my community and minister the gospel to those who have not yet accepted the Lord." Everyone nodded enthusiastically.

"I would dedicate all of my remaining time to serving God, my family, my church, and my fellow man," a woman added. Everyone murmured approval.

After several similar comments, one man broke from the pack and said, "I would go to my mother-in-law's house for the four weeks."

The room got very quiet. Finally the leader asked, "Why your mother-in-law's home?"

"Because that would be the longest four weeks of my life!" the man replied.

The Bible's
teaching about the
Second Coming does
a lot more than warn us
against foolish living. Many
verses that speak of the
return of Christ do so in
order to encourage us
and give us strength
when tough times hit.
For example,
our bodies fail us;
that's just a fact. They
get tired, get old, get
injured, get sick.
Those who suffer from
chronic pain know all
about discouraging days. And those
who suffer with terminal illnesses
know all about their mortality. So
it lifts our spirits when we read,
"We are citizens of heaven, where
the Lord Jesus Christ lives. And we
are eagerly waiting for him to return
as our Savior. He will take these weak
mortal bodies of ours and change them
into glorious bodies like his own, using
the same mighty power that he will use
to conquer everything, everywhere"
(Philippians 3:20-21).

You, too, must be patient. And take courage, for the coming of the Lord is near" (James 5:7-8).

❝❝ He SAiD It ❞❞

The greatest power is often simple patience.

ELI JOSEPH COSSMAN

Millions of Christians across the centuries have felt the sting of religious persecution, many of them choosing to give up their lives rather than turn their backs on Christ. The Bible uses the certainty of Christ's return to encourage them in dark days: "God will provide rest for you who are being persecuted and also for us when the Lord Jesus appears from heaven. He will come with his mighty angels, in flaming fire, bringing judgment on those who don't know God and on those who refuse to obey the Good News of our Lord Jesus" (2 Thessalonians 1:7-8).

Or how about believers who just feel tired of waiting? Their difficult lives tempt them to demand that Jesus come back, *right now*. The Bible also has a word for them: "Dear brothers and sisters, you must be patient as you wait for the Lord's return. Consider the farmers who eagerly look for the rains in the fall and in the spring. They patiently wait for the precious harvest to ripen.

The MeDia CoVeRS the EnD of the WoRLD

USA Today: WE'RE DEAD

Wall Street Journal: Dow Plummets as World Ends

National Enquirer: Elvis Spotted with the Real King

Inc. Magazine: 10 Ways You Can Profit from the Apocalypse

Rolling Stone: The Grateful Dead Reunion Tour

Ladies' Home Journal: Lose 10 Pounds by Judgment Day with Our New "Armageddon" Diet!

Sports Illustrated: Game Over

The certainty of Jesus' return can give you great encouragement in tough times.

THe BoOK of ReVeLaTioN, ABRiDGeD

- Look! He comes with the clouds of heaven. And everyone will see him (1:7).
- "Look, I am coming quickly. Hold on to what you have so that no one will take away your crown" (3:11).
- "Look, I am coming soon! Blessed are those who obey the prophecy written in this scroll" (22:7).
- "See, I am coming soon, and my reward is with me, to repay all according to their deeds" (22:12).
- He who is the faithful witness to all these things says, "Yes, I am coming soon!" Amen! Come, Lord Jesus (22:20)!

Evangelist Billy Graham carefully considered these passages and concluded, "I've read the last page of the Bible. It's all going to turn out all right."[2]

He SAiD It

Live as though Jesus is coming any moment, but plan as though you have 100 years!

DICK MILLS

Pondering the return of Jesus can change our lives in countless positive ways—exactly what God had in mind when He inspired the hundreds of Bible passages that predict the Second Coming of Christ.

Even the quality of our friendships can skyrocket when we meditate on the return of Christ. Paul wrote to some special friends, "What gives us hope and joy, and what is our proud reward and crown? It is you! Yes, you will bring us much joy as we stand together before our Lord Jesus when he comes back again. For you are our pride and joy" (1 Thessalonians 2:19-20). As the apostle looked into the future, he saw Jesus coming back—and his friends right by his side, grinning ear to ear. The thought made him love his friends even more than he did before. And there's no reason the same thing can't happen for you!

Contemplating the Second Coming also helps us to rein in our ugly tendency to judge others. The Bible says, "So be careful not to jump to conclusions before the Lord returns as to whether or not someone is faithful. When the Lord comes, he will bring our deepest secrets to light and will reveal our private motives. And then God will give to everyone whatever praise is due" (1 Corinthians 4:5; see also Romans 14:9-13).

Many wonderful things happen when we think about the return of Jesus—at least, so long as we ponder it as God intended. Perhaps the biggest benefit of all is that it gives us encouragement to keep growing: "And let us . . . encourage and warn each other, especially now that the day of his coming back again is drawing near" (Hebrews 10:25).

Jesus is coming back! When? Who knows? But perhaps today!

By meditating on the return of Jesus, *you* can find the confidence to live well (see 1 John 2:28).

By meditating on the return of Jesus, *you* can find the motivation to live a life that honors God (see 2 Peter 3:10-12; 1 John 3:2-3).

By meditating on the return of Jesus, *you* can be ready for that moment when the long wait ends and you "will see the Son of Man arrive on the clouds of heaven with power and great glory" (Matthew 24:30). What an amazing day that will be! On that awesome day, all of God's people will feel a depth of joy they had never even imagined. On that day God "will bring you into his glorious presence innocent of sin and with great joy" (Jude 24).

But you know what? You don't have to wait until Jesus returns to start feeling a little of that kind of joy *right now*. God designed the growing Christian life to give you a foretaste of the fabulous things He's planned for you—and you can start enjoying them today, regardless of your current circumstances.

THE RAPTURE...
a one-way,
all-expense-paid
trip for all
eternity...
NO BAGGAGE ALLOWED.

KEEP
LOOKING UP...
GOD IS LOOKING
DOWN.

RAPTURE
...separation of
Church & State.

So What?

👉 Regularly pondering the return of Christ brings a serious (and joyful!) focus to your life.

👉 A wise emphasis on the Second Coming can radically improve your home, church, and interpersonal experiences.

👉 By focusing on the reality of Christ's return, you find great encouragement in difficult times.

SHeEP TaLK

Lord, help me to remember every moment of my life that Jesus Christ is coming back to earth . . . maybe even today! Show me what it takes to get ready for His return, and please keep me from ever treating the Second Coming merely as some quaint doctrine or as a topic for silly speculation. As I read Your Word, let the return of Christ come alive for me in ways I've never experienced, and use that experience to make me more eager to live and work in a way that pleases You. In Jesus' name, amen.

---

1. The first coming of Christ—when He was born in Bethlehem about two thousand years ago—is mentioned some 129 times.

2. http://www.brainyquote.com/quotes/quotes/b/billygraha150656.html

HoW to eNJoY a TaSTe oF HeaVeN

Cherry pie. Double-chocolate-fudge premium ice cream. Fresh, homemade bread. A thick, juicy steak, grilled to perfection. A sweet, crisp apple. A gourmet hot dog on a gorgeous summer afternoon, piled high with all the condiments you love.

Are you salivating yet?

Our sense of taste has to be one of God's most exquisite gifts to us. It brings us joy by the mouthful and helps us to appreciate the amazing creativity of our Maker. To taste something delicious reminds us of the goodness of God.

In your spiritual life, are you tasting the goodness of God? He promises His people joy, peace, and newness of life—are you tasting these heavenly goodies right now? If you're not, or if you're not tasting them as much as you'd like, you can do something about it. You really can enjoy a foretaste of heaven while still living on earth.

❝ SHe SAiD It ❞

As with most fine things, chocolate has its season. There is a simple memory aid that you can use to determine whether it is the correct time to order chocolate dishes: any month whose name contains the letter A, E, or U is the proper time for chocolate.

SANDRA BOYNTON

So what does heaven "taste" like? How do we know when we take in a mouthful?

One of the chief characteristics of heaven is that everything there is new. Old and dilapidated, you won't find. Dried up and crumbling, nowhere to be seen. "Then I saw a *new* heaven and *new* earth," writes John, "for the old heaven and the old earth had disappeared . . .

And I saw. . . the *new* Jerusalem, coming down from God out of heaven like a beautiful bride prepared for her husband . . . And the one sitting on the throne said, 'Look, I am making *all things new!*'" (Revelation 21:1-2, 5, emphasis added).

The great day John described has not yet arrived, but already God is busy making old things new. To every Christian He has given:

➤ a new heart and a new spirit
(see Ezekiel 18:31; 11:19; 36:26).

➤ new birth (see 1 Peter 1:3).

➤ a new life (see Acts 5:20; Romans 6:14).

➤ a new mind (see Ephesians 4:23).

➤ a new name (see Isaiah 62:2; Revelation 2:17).

God has given every one of us:

➤ a new nature (see Ephesians 4:24; Colossians 3:10).

And has made us into:

➤ and a new creation (see 2 Corinthians 5:17; Galatians 6:15).

Because of all of this, He has given us new songs to sing (see Psalm 33:3; 40:3; 96:1; 98:1; 144:9; Isaiah 42:10; Revelation 5:9; 14:3).

Have you begun to sing those new songs that put a taste of heaven in your mouth? Have the melodies of heaven begun to lift your heart to the throne of God?

SoMeONe YoU SHoULD KNoW

In his day, Philips Brooks (1835-1893) was widely regarded as one of the premier preachers in America. He served as rector of Trinity Episcopal Church in Boston and is most remembered today for writing the popular Christmas carol "O Little Town of Bethlehem."

Brooks thought not only about the birth of Christ, however; he also pondered what life ought to be like with God, right here and right now. He wrote, "The great danger facing all of us . . . is . . . that some day we may wake up and find that always we have been busy with husks and trappings of life and have really missed life itself. For life without God, to one who has known the richness and joy of life with Him, is unthinkable, impossible. That is what one prays one's friends may be spared—satisfaction with a life that falls short of the best, that has in it no tingle or thrill that comes from a friendship with the Father."[1]

❝ SoMeONe ❞ SAiD It

Sing like no one is listening, dance like no one is watching, love like you'll never get hurt, and live like it's heaven on earth.

UNKNOWN

God is busy making your whole life into something new.

If heaven puts one overarching feeling into the hearts of all its residents, it has to be joy. Heaven is a very joyful place!

Since God is there, how could overpowering joy not follow? In heaven we will know the unequaled joy of God's presence and the pleasures of living with Him forever (see Psalm 16:11). There is a reason why in heaven you will join "thousands of angels in joyful assembly" (Hebrews 12:22)!

💬 SoMEoNe 💬 SAiD It

Anyone can sing in the sunshine. You and I should sing on when the sun has gone down, or when clouds pour out their rain, for Christ is with us.

UNKNOWN

In heaven we will experience full and uninterrupted joy—but even now we can get a taste of it. Peter said to some Christian friends, "Even now you are happy with a glorious, inexpressible joy" (1 Peter 1:8). Paul said that the Kingdom of God is a matter of "joy in the Holy Spirit" (Romans 14:17) and he prayed that God "will keep you happy and full of peace as you believe in him" (Romans 15:13).

This kind of joy doesn't depend on outside circumstances. Even in dark times, you can taste a little of heaven's joy. That was the experience of a group of Christians in Paul's day, to whom he wrote, "You received the message with joy from the Holy Spirit in spite of the severe suffering it brought you" (1 Thessalonians 1:6; see also 2 Corinthians 7:4).

Do you know the taste of heaven's joy? When was the last time it tickled your spiritual taste buds?

Yee-HAW!

A pastor died and found himself waiting in line at the Pearly Gates. Ahead of him stood a guy dressed in sunglasses, a loud shirt, leather jacket, and jeans. Soon Saint Peter arrived and asked the casually dressed man, "Who are you? I need to know whether to admit you to heaven."

"I'm David Silverburg," the man said, "taxi driver, of Noo Yawk City."

Saint Peter consulted his list, smiled, and said to the cab driver, "Take this silken robe and golden staff and enter heaven." The man did so and vanished down a golden street.

Then it was the pastor's turn. Without waiting to be addressed, he stood tall, puffed out his chest, and declared, "I am Robert James, pastor of Our Redeemer for the last thirty-nine years."

After checking his list, Saint Peter said to the pastor, "Take this cotton robe and wooden staff and enter heaven."

Saint Peter's unexpected words shook the pastor and he objected, "Just a moment here. That man was a cab driver—and he got a silken robe and golden staff. How can this be?"

"Up here," replied the smiling apostle, "results are what get the rewards. While you preached, people slept; while he drove, people prayed."

Heaven is also a place of total and satisfying peace. Worry will not exist. Neither will conflict or fighting or hatred. God will remove all of our sorrows, "and there will be no more death or sorrow or crying or pain" (Revelation 21:4). Best of all, the Prince of Peace, Jesus Christ, will take His throne, and "his ever-expanding, peaceful government will never end" (Isaiah 9:7).

Despite living on this very unpeaceful planet, we can still taste a little of heaven's peace right now. "God wants his children to live in peace," the Bible says (1 Corinthians 7:15). Jesus told us, "I am leaving you with a gift—peace of mind and heart" (John 14:27). And God's Word leaves us with a reassuring prayer: "May the Lord of peace himself always give you his peace no matter what happens" (2 Thessalonians 3:16).

SHe SAiD It

I do not want the peace that passeth understanding.
I want the understanding which bringeth peace.

HELEN KELLER

It says that God will bless you with His "wonderful peace *as you come to know* Jesus, our God and Lord, better and better" (2 Peter 1:2, emphasis added). It tells you to pray about everything rather than worrying about anything so that "you will experience God's peace, which is far more wonderful than the human mind can understand. His peace will guard your hearts and minds *as you live in Christ Jesus*" (Philippians 4:7, emphasis added).

Enjoying that peace isn't automatic, however. The Bible says, "*If* the Holy Spirit controls your mind, there is life and peace" (Romans 8:6, emphasis added). It says, "*Let* the peace that comes from Christ rule in your hearts" (Colossians 3:15, emphasis added).

He SAiD It

The main object of religion is not to get a man into heaven, but to get heaven into him.

THOMAS HARDY

God equips you to experience some of heaven's peace right here on earth.

While God wants us to experience a little bit of heaven even while we still live on a sinful and trouble-filled earth, many of us have a problem—a big one. We hear these promises of life and joy and peace, and yet we rarely experience them. Much of the time, we feel like Paul as he described his own life: "We are pressed on every side by troubles . . . We are perplexed . . . We are hunted down . . . We get knocked down . . . Through suffering, these bodies of ours constantly share in the death of Jesus . . . We live under constant danger of death . . . We live in the face of death" (2 Corinthians 4:8-12).

Where is the life?

Where is the joy?

Where is the peace?

❝ He SAiD It ❞

A little faith will bring your soul to heaven;
A great faith will bring heaven to your soul.

CHARLES SPURGEON

Paul didn't deny his troubles, but neither did he give up on tasting the delicacies of heaven despite his troubles. He insisted, "We never give up. Though our bodies are dying, our spirits are being renewed every day. For our present troubles are quite small and won't last very long. Yet they produce for us an immeasurably great glory that will last forever! So we don't look at the troubles we can see right now; rather, we look forward to what we have not yet seen. For the troubles we see will soon be over, but the joys to come will last forever" (2 Corinthians 4:16-18).

How did Paul manage to taste heaven even while still on earth? Through faith. And that's the key for you, too.

TaKe A LiTTLe TiMe

➢ Set your stopwatch: how many good things can you name about God in ten seconds?

➢ Get a piece of paper: how many good things can you write down about God in five minutes?

➢ Close your eyes: praise God for His goodness, out loud, for ten minutes.

Faith is like a pair of eyeglasses. It gives you spiritual vision so that you can function better and enjoy life more. Faith is not the practice of closing your eyes and walking around in the dark, trusting that you won't fall off a cliff. Faith is a way to fix your eyes on what is unseen and eternal.

Throughout your life on this earth, you will have a choice to make: will you see everything that happens to you through the lens of faith, or will you interpret all of your circumstances through the lens of unfaith? The lens of faith enables you to see God everywhere, not just here and there. The lens of unfaith can't see God anywhere. Which lens you choose to use—and it is a daily choice—will make a profound difference in the quality and effectiveness of your life.

❝ SHe SAiD It ❞

Let God's promises shine on your problems.

CORRIE TEN BOOM

When good stuff happens, faith says, "God has blessed me with this"—and you get a taste of life and joy and peace. Unfaith says, "I made this happen," or "It happened by chance"—and the taste of heaven eludes you.

When bad stuff happens, faith says, "I don't like it, but I will still trust God"—and a little bit of heaven seeps through. Unfaith says, "Either there is no God, or He doesn't care"—and life and joy and peace evaporate.

The same thing takes place when fun stuff or hard stuff or ordinary stuff or confusing stuff happens. If you look at these things through the lens of faith, you can get a taste of heaven. If you look at them through the lens of unfaith, you get a mouthful of gravel. You can put on the glasses of faith or keep them off.

But do you want to be blessed? Do you want to taste a little bit of heaven? Then you have no choice. You have to put on those glasses of faith and through them look at everything that life throws at you.

Every day you interpret your life through either the lens of faith or unfaith.

THe STReNGtH oF FaiTH

Faith is the very first thing you should pack in a hope chest.

SARAH BAN BREATHNACH

You can do very little with faith, but you can do nothing without it.

SAMUEL BUTLER

He who loses money, loses much; he who loses a friend, loses much more; he who loses faith, loses all.

ELEANOR ROOSEVELT

❝ He SAiD It ❞

The more I considered Christianity, the more I found that while it had established a rule and order, the chief aim of that order was to give room for good things to run wild.

G. K. CHESTERTON

What have you tasted so far of the goodness of God? What exotic flavors of His grace make you break into a broad smile? He throws a magnificent banquet for you, even in the presence of your enemies, and invites you to eat and enjoy to the fullest (see Psalm 23).

Are you taking advantage of all the good things your heavenly Father wants to give you? Despite your troubles, despite your hardships, despite your hurts or difficulties or problems—are you learning how to taste a little bit of heaven right now, right where God has placed you? And are you helping others to taste the same heavenly delicacies? For that really is God's plan for you. He says to you, today, even as He always says to His dearly loved sons and daughters:

"Taste and see that the LORD is good. Oh, the joys of those who trust in him!" (Psalm 34:8)

❝ SoMeoNe ❞ SAiD It

I asked God for all things, that I might enjoy life.
God gave life, that I might enjoy all things.

UNKNOWN

So What?

☞ God invites you to experience *right now* some of the newness, joy, and peace of heaven by exercising your faith.

☞ Every day and every moment, you choose whether you will see your life through the lens of faith or unfaith.

☞ How much of heaven you taste on earth is largely up to you.

SHeEP TaLK

Lord, thank You for inviting me to taste a little bit of heaven even while I still live on earth. Help me to fully enjoy all the items on the great menu You provide, but also show me how to become a the kind of waiter who can help others to taste and enjoy Your delicacies as well. Thank You for Your joy! Thank You for Your peace! Thank you for giving me new life and a new outlook and a new hope! But most of all, Lord, thank You for giving Yourself to me, free and without cost. I love You, Lord! In Jesus' name, amen.

1. http://trinityboston.org/wsp_smn_smnpage.asp?docpage=20020120.html

WHaT DoeS THaT MeaN?

A

Abraham — A "man of faith" and friend of God who lived about 4,000 years ago. By trusting God and His promises, Abraham became the father of the Jewish people and still serves as a great example of how to become a person of faith.

See Genesis 11:27—25:11; Exodus 3:6; Isaiah 41:8; Romans 4:1-25; Galatians 3:6-18; Hebrews 6:12-15; 11:8-19; James 2:21-23.

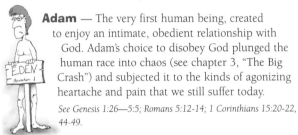

Adam — The very first human being, created to enjoy an intimate, obedient relationship with God. Adam's choice to disobey God plunged the human race into chaos (see chapter 3, "The Big Crash") and subjected it to the kinds of agonizing heartache and pain that we still suffer today.

See Genesis 1:26—5:5; Romans 5:12-14; 1 Corinthians 15:20-22, 44-49.

Apostles — The earliest leaders of the Christians, sent and authorized by God to direct the affairs of the young Church (the name "apostle" means "sent one") and to perform miraculous signs of many kinds. Most of the apostles had been with Jesus before His crucifixion; at least one apostle, Paul, saw Jesus not in His earthly body, but in a vision.

See Matthew 10:2-4; Mark 3:14; Acts 2:42-43; 4:33; 5:12; 14:14; Romans 16:7; 1 Corinthians 12:28; 2 Corinthians 12:12; Galatians 2:8; Ephesians 2:19-20.

B

Barnabas — A leader and apostle in the early church, known for encouraging believers. He is responsible for introducing Paul to the church and for helping him to gain acceptance there. He often accompanied Paul on his travels.

See Acts 4:36; 9:26-28; 11:22-26; 13:1—15:39; 1 Corinthians 9:6; Galatians 2:1, 9, 13.

Bible — A unique book, supernaturally inspired by God, that tells us how to enjoy a rewarding and successful life of faith. It consists of 66 smaller books—39 in the Old Testament, 27 in the New Testament—written by more than forty authors over many centuries. It is often also called the Word of God or the Scriptures. To make it easier for readers to find specific passages in the Bible, many years ago scholars added chapter and verse designations to the text. "John 3:16," for example, points readers to the book of John in the New Testament, then to a portion of the book labeled chapter 3, then to an even smaller portion designated verse sixteen.

See John 10:35; Acts 6:2; Ephesians 6:17; 2 Timothy 3:16-17; Hebrews 4:12; 2 Peter 1:20-21.

Big Crash — The disobedience of Adam and Eve in the garden of Eden caused a terrible fracture in their relationship with God and prompted Him to subject the earth to harsh and painful conditions, including death (see chapter 3, "The Big Crash"). The Big Crash continues to plague the earth and its residents today.

See Genesis 3:1-24; Isaiah 13:9-13; 24:20; Romans 8:18-25.

C

Christian — A name given by first-century observers to those who had decided to place their faith in Jesus Christ. The term literally means "follower of Christ" or even "little Christ."

See Acts 11:26; 26:28; 1 Peter 4:16.

Church — The name given to groups of believers in Christ who regularly gather for worship, service, encouragement and instruction. It does not refer to a building or facility, but to the assembled congregation of men and women, boys and girls, who have placed their faith in Jesus. It is also often called the Body of Christ or the family of God.

See Matthew 16:18; Acts 8:1; 9:31; 13:1; 14:23, 27; 18:22; 20:17; Romans 16:1; 1 Corinthians 14:12; Ephesians 1:22-23; 5:25-32; Colossians 1:18, 24; 1 Timothy 3:15.

Cross — A wooden tool of execution, shaped like a small "t," a capital "T" or an "X." Victims were affixed to the cross, which stood upright, and left to die. In the Roman Empire, such an execution was usually reserved for slaves, non-citizens and the worst of criminals.

See Mark 15:32; John 19:17-19; Acts 2:23; 1 Corinthians 1:18; Galatians 6:14; Philippians 2:8; Colossians 2:13-15; Hebrews 12:2.

Crucifixion or **Crucify** — A brutal form of execution perfected by the ancient Romans. Usually reserved for criminals or enemies of the state, it involved attaching a condemned man to a wooden cross (either by nails or rope), then allowing him to die either of exposure or asphyxiation. The Romans executed Jesus Christ using this barbaric procedure.

See Matthew 20:17-19; 27:26, 38; John 19:10-11; Acts 2:36; 1 Corinthians 1:23; 2:8; Revelation 11:8.

Curse — A pronouncement of divine judgment that results in painful and serious consequences for the ones judged. God "cursed" both individuals and the earth when Adam and Eve disobeyed His explicit instructions. And Jesus Christ "became a curse" for believers when He willingly died on the cross to take the punishment that they had earned through their sin.

See Genesis 3:14-19; 4:11; 5:29; 8:21; Proverbs 3:33; Isaiah 24:6; 1 Corinthians 16:22; Galatians 3:10, 13; Revelation 22:3.

D

David — The second king of ancient Israel, David took the throne about a thousand years before the birth of Christ. He was known as "Israel's singer of songs" and wrote many of the songs found in the Bible's book of Psalms. He founded a dynasty that eventually produced Jesus Christ, the "Son of David" and the Savior of the world.

See 1 Samuel 16 — 1 Kings 2; 1 Chronicles 2 — 29; 2 Samuel 23:1; Isaiah 16:5; Matthew 1:1; 9:27; Acts 2:24-36; 13:22-23; 2 Timothy 2:8-9; Revelation 5:5; 22:16.

Devil — See "Satan."

Disciple — A follower of Jesus Christ who faithfully learns and practices whatever lessons God may give him or her. A disciple commits himself or herself to hearing Jesus' Word and then doing it, by faith.

See Matthew 5:1-2; 27:57; Luke 14:25-33; John 19:38; Acts 6:1; 9:1, 10, 26, 36.

E

Eden — A beautiful ancient garden, the original Paradise, created to be the home of Adam and Eve. When they disobeyed God, they were forcibly ejected from Eden and prevented from ever living there again.

See Genesis 2:8-17; 3:23-24; Isaiah 51:3; Ezekiel 36:35-36.

Eternal life — A joy-filled, peaceful, and fruitful existence, given by God to believers in Jesus, that lasts forever. It begins the moment a person places his or her faith in Christ and reaches its full and greatest expression in heaven.

See Matthew 19:16-30; 25:31-46; John 3:16, 36; 4:13-14; 5:24; 6:40; 10:27-28; 17:1-3; Acts 13:46, 48; Romans 2:7; 6:23; Galatians 6:8; 1 John 5:13.

Eve — The first woman, created by God as a "helper," wife, and companion for Adam. Satan tricked her into disobeying God and she convinced her husband to join her in her disobedience. As a result, the pair saddled their descendants (including us) with a cursed world.

See Genesis 3:1-20; 4:1; 2 Corinthians 11:3; 1 Timothy 2:13-14.

F

Faith — A firm belief in the trustworthiness of God that prompts someone to stake his or her whole life on the promises of God. It combines belief with commitment and results in personal action consistent with God's revealed will.

See Matthew 9:29; 13:58; 21:21; Acts 3:16; 6:7; 20:21; Romans 1:5; 3:22—5:2; 10:9-10, 17; 1 Corinthians 15:14-17; 2 Corinthians 5:7; 10:15; Galatians 2:16.

Fellowship — The delightful experience of community that God intends for believers in Christ to enjoy whenever they connect with God or gather together under the banner of Jesus.

See Acts 2:42; 1 Corinthians 1:9; Galatians 2:9; Philippians 2:1; 3:10; 1 John 1:3, 6-7.

Forbidden fruit — The fruit of the "tree of the knowledge of good and evil" growing in the Garden of Eden. God told Adam not to eat this fruit, and when he disobeyed, chaos resulted (see chapter 3, "The Big Crash").

See Genesis 2:15-17; 3:1-19.

Forgiveness — The granting of a pardon for an offense clearly committed. When God forgives someone, all that person's sins get wiped clean. When we forgive others, we clear the way for the restoration of a damaged relationship.

See Psalm 130:4; Matthew 26:28; Luke 24:45-47; Acts 2:38; 5:31; 10:43; 13:38-39; Ephesians 1:7-8; Colossians 1:13-14; 3:13.

G

Glory — A shorthand way of referring to the awesome power and majesty and greatness and beauty of God. Glory makes us gasp and say, "Wow!" God says that He plans to one day share His glory with believers in Christ.

See Exodus 15:11; 33:18—34:8; Psalm 19:1-6; Isaiah 6:3; Matthew 16:27; Romans 3:23; 8:17-18; 1 Corinthians 10:31; 2 Corinthians 3:18; Revelation 21:23.

Glossary — A collection of difficult or obscure terms, defined and/or described using more familiar terms; a short dictionary or lexicon; a feature called "What Does That Mean?".

See Nehemiah 8:7-8; Ecclesiastes 6:11; 1 Corinthians 14:11.

God the Father — The Supreme Being, Creator of the universe, the first Person of the Trinity, and the Ruler of all. Not a mere impersonal force or abstract principle, but a living Being with a personality and emotions and a will. Jesus referred to Him as "My Father" and instructed His followers to call Him "Our Father."

See Matthew 6:9; 11:27; John 3:35; 20:17; Romans 6:4; 1 Corinthians 8:6; 15:24; 2 Corinthians 1:3-4; Ephesians 3:14-15;1 Timothy 6:15-16; Hebrews 12:7-11.

God's Word — See "Bible."

H

Heart — The core of one's being, the essence of a person. In the Bible, it almost never refers to the physical organ that pumps blood through the body, but rather to the inner life and central part of an individual's existence and character.

See Genesis 6:5; Joshua 22:5; 1 Samuel 12:24; Jeremiah 17:9-10; 24:7; 29:13; Ezekiel 11:19-20; Matthew 6:21; Acts 16:14; Colossians 3:23.

Heaven — The eternal home of God and the final home of all believers in Christ. A place of infinite love, peace, joy, and purity, where nothing evil or impure can ever enter.

See Genesis 28:12; Psalm 2:4; 14:2; 115:3; Colossians 4:1; 1 Thessalonians 1:10; Hebrews 8:1-2; 9:24; James 3:17; 2 Peter 3:13; Revelation 21:27.

Holy — Anything morally pure, separate from all evil, and reflecting the absolute purity of God. Since believers are "holy" because they have been united to Christ by faith, they are to live in a way that reflects God's own purity.

See Exodus 19:23; 1 Samuel 2:2; Psalm 89:7; 2 Timothy 1:8-9; 2 Timothy 2:20-21; Hebrews 10:10, 14; 12:14; 1 Peter 1:14-16; 2:9; 2 Peter 3:11-12; Revelation 4:8.

Holy Spirit — The third Person of the Trinity who, along with God the Father and God the Son, makes up the one-and-only Godhead. He indwells all believers in Christ and gives them the power to live in a way that pleases God.

See Genesis 1:2; Psalm 51:11; Isaiah 63:10-11; Matthew 1:18; Mark 12:36; Luke 4:1; 11:13; John 14:26; 15:26; 16:7-15; Acts 1:8; Romans 5:5; Titus 3:5-6.

Hope — A confident expectation that God will fulfill all His promises, even when life looks most grim. It is not mere positive thinking, but a rock-solid conviction that, in the end, everything will turn out amazingly well, just as God said.

See Psalm 25:3-5; Isaiah 40:30-31; Jeremiah 29:11; Romans 4:18; 5:1-5; 8:22-25; 15:4, 13; 2 Corinthians 1:10; Hebrews 6:16-20; 10:23; 1 Peter 1:13.

I

Image of God — In this way all men and women stand apart from the animals, since only humans are made in God's image—that is, in His likeness. We mirror our Creator in many (but not all!) significant ways. Therefore, all humans have tremendous worth and value.

See Genesis 1:26-27; 5:1; 9:6; 1 Corinthians 11:7; Colossians 3:10; James 3:9-10.

Israel — The name given to the nation and kingdom of the ancient Hebrews, the "chosen people" of God. Jacob, the son of Abraham, was given this name after a memorable encounter with God, and later the name came to be associated with all his descendants. The name means "he strives with God."

See Genesis 32:28; 35:10; Exodus 3:16; 5:1-2; Isaiah 5:7; Matthew 2:6, 20; 19:28; Acts 5:31; Romans 9:1-9, 27-29; 11:25-29; Galatians 6:16; Ephesians 2:11-22.

J

James — One of the original apostles, the half-brother of Jesus, and a crucial leader in the early Jerusalem church. During Jesus' lifetime, James apparently did not believe in Him, but after the resurrection, he came to place his faith in Jesus. He is credited with writing the book of James in the New Testament.

See Mark 6:3; Acts 12:17; 15:13; 21:18; 1 Corinthians 15:7; Galatians 1:19; 2:12.

Jerusalem — The capital of ancient Israel and the city where Jesus Christ was crucified. King Solomon built the temple there around 973 B.C. Also called Zion, Jerusalem holds a large and important place in Bible history and prophecy and continues to make headlines today.

See Joshua 10:1; 2 Samuel 5:6-7; 2 Chronicles 36:23; Psalm 51:18; Daniel 1:1-2; Zechariah 12:2-6; Matthew 2:1-3; 5:35; Luke 2:22-25; Acts 1:4-8; Revelation 21:2.

Jesus Christ — The second Person of the Trinity who, along with God the Father and the Holy Spirit, makes up the one-and-only Godhead. Although eternally God, He became a human in order to die for our sins and rose from the dead on the third day after His crucifixion, thus proving His identity. The Old Testament features hundreds of prophecies about His life, while the four Gospels (Matthew, Mark, Luke, and John) in the New Testament describe many events in His life and the rest of the New Testament provides commentary on it. He is often called both "Savior" and "Lord."

See Genesis 3:15; Deuteronomy 18:15; 2 Samuel 7:11-16; Psalm 22; Isaiah 52:13—53:12; Micah 5:2; Romans 1:1-4; 1 Corinthians 15:1-8; Revelation 1:5.

John — One of the original apostles, John may be considered Jesus' closest earthly friend. On the cross, Jesus committed the care of His elderly mother to John. John is credited with writing the New Testament books of John, the epistles of John, and the Revelation.

See Matthew 4:21-22; 10:2; 17:1-2; Mark 3:17; 5:37; Luke 9:51-56; Acts 1:13; 3:1-10; 4:1-4; Galatians 2:9; John 13:23; 19:26; 20:2; 21:7, 20; Revelation 22:8.

L

Law — A set of commands and instructions given by God to His people, especially those received by Moses. Since no one (other than Jesus) can completely obey the Law, it has no power to save anyone. Those who place their faith in Jesus are credited with the spotless record of Christ.

See Exodus 24:12; Deuteronomy 1:5; 4:44-46; Psalm 119:1; Luke 10:25-28; Romans 2:12-27; 3:19-28; 8:1-4; 13:8-10; 1 Corinthians 15:56; Galatians 3:10-13.

Lord — In the Old Testament, "Lord" is usually a reference to God Almighty. In the New Testament, it usually refers to Jesus but may also refer to God the Father. It means "master, sovereign, boss" and often describes deity.

See Genesis 2:4; Proverbs 28:14; Isaiah 3:1; Matthew 1:20; Luke 24:34; John 20:28; Acts 1:21, 24; 2:36; Romans 1:4, 7; 7:25; 10:9; 1 Corinthians 16:22-23.

Lord's Supper — Just hours before His crucifixion, Jesus led His disciples in a final meal that foreshadowed both His impending death for the sins of the world and His eventual return at the Second Coming. He instructed His followers to regularly celebrate this simple meal, called the "Lord's Supper," both to remember His death and to prepare for His return.

See Matthew 26:17-30; Mark 14:12-26; Luke 22:7-20; John 13:21-30; 1 Corinthians 10:16; 11:17-33.

M

Moses — Known primarily as the "lawgiver of Israel," Moses received the Ten Commandments from God and delivered them to his people. He led the ancient Israelites out of Egyptian slavery, then led them in the wilderness for forty years afterwards. While God did not allow Moses to enter the Promised Land because of an act of public disobedience, centuries later he had the privilege of briefly meeting with Jesus on what is known as the Mount of Transfiguration.

See Exodus 2:1—4:18; 20:1-20; Numbers 20:6-12; Deuteronomy 34:1-8; Mark 9:1-10; Luke 24:25-27; John 1:17; 5:45-47; Acts 7:17-50; Hebrews 3:4-6; 11:24-29.

N

New nature — A new disposition and eagerness to do what pleases God, in contrast to the old nature that craves to do only what pleases itself.

To everyone who places his or her faith in Christ, God gives this "new nature," enabling the person to delight in God and His ways.

See Romans 6:4; 2 Corinthians 5:17; Galatians 6:15; Ephesians 4:23-24; Colossians 3:10; 1 Peter 1:3.

New Testament — Roughly the last one-fifth of the Bible, the New Testament begins with the four Gospels (Matthew, Mark, Luke, and John all highlight several key episodes from the earthly life of Jesus) and ends with the book of Revelation, which highlights the worldwide triumph of God and the reign of Christ. It consists of 27 books, all written within a few decades of the resurrection of Jesus.

See Matthew—Revelation.

O

Old nature — Everyone born into this world arrives with a powerful selfish inclination, a strong inward tendency to value personal desires over the ones expressed by God. The Bible says that we inherited this evil tendency from Adam and that, on our own, we cannot break its power over us. The old nature leads inevitably to death.

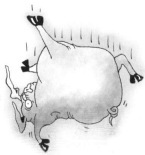

See Romans 7:5, 18, 25; 8:3-14; 13:14; 1 Corinthians 5:5; Galatians 5:13-24; 6:8; Ephesians 2:3; Colossians 2:11, 13: 3:5; 2 Peter 2:10, 18.

Old Testament — Roughly the first four-fifths of the Bible, the Old Testament begins with the book of Genesis and ends with the book of Malachi. It highlights God's dealings with Abraham's descendants, the Hebrews, and sets the stage for the arrival of Jesus Christ, the Savior of the world.

See Genesis—Malachi.

P

Paul — A Jewish man of the first century who had a dramatic conversion to faith in Christ and who did more to spread Christianity throughout the world, especially among non-Jews, than perhaps anyone in history. Before his conversion, Paul (then known as Saul) tried to destroy the young church by persecuting and imprisoning its members. He is credited with writing at least thirteen of the books of the New Testament.

See Acts 7:57—8:3; 9:1-31; 20:17-38; Romans 1:1; 11:13; 1 Corinthians 9:1-2; 15:9-10; Galatians 1:13—2:14; 1 Timothy 2:7; 2 Peter 3:15-16.

Peter — The recognized leader of the original twelve disciples of Jesus and formerly a professional fisherman who lived in the coastal town of Capernaum. Along with James and John, he formed the inner circle of Jesus' closest friends. He concentrated his ministry among his Jewish countrymen but also argued forcefully that God offered eternal life to all people, regardless of their ethnic backgrounds. He is credited with writing 1 and 2 Peter in the New Testament.

See Matthew 4:18-20; 14:25-33; 16:13-23; 17:1-9; Luke 22:31-62; 24:11-12; John 20:3-10; 21:1-19; Acts 1:13-22; 2:14-41; 3:1—4:31; 10:1-48; Galatians 2:7-8.

Prayer — A dynamic, two-way communication with God in which believers pour out their hearts in praise, confession, petition, and intercession, then watch for His response. In prayer we ask God for things we need, admit our faults, and rejoice in who He is.

See Genesis 20:7; Deuteronomy 4:7; 2 Chronicles 7:14; Psalm 5:2; Matthew 6:5-13; Luke 6:12; 22:39-46; Romans 8:26-27; Ephesians 6:18-19; 1 Thessalonians 5:17.

Promised Land — A large piece of real estate that God promised on oath to give to the descendants of Abraham. The territory ranged from the Mediterranean Sea on the west to the Nile River on the south to the Euphrates River on the north— the ancient land of Canaan.

See Genesis 15:7-21; 17:7-8; Exodus 3:17; Deuteronomy 34:1-4; Joshua 1:1-4; Judges 2:20-23; 1 Chronicles 16:16-18; Hebrews 11:9.

Prophecy or prophet — A prophet is one who speaks the words of God, just as God inspires the person to speak them. A prophecy is the divinely inspired utterance that the prophet speaks, often including a prediction of some future event. Since anyone can claim to speak for God, the Bible gives several tests to identify bogus prophets.

See Numbers 12:6; Deuteronomy 13:1-5; 18:20-22; Jeremiah 23:9-40; Acts 2:16-37; 7:37; 13:6; 21:10-14; 1 Corinthians 14:1-5; 14:37; 1 John 4:1-3.

Psalmist — We do not know who wrote many of the chapters in the book of Psalms found in the Old Testament. One way to refer to the unknown author of a psalm is to call him "the psalmist."

See Psalm 1; 2; 10; 33; 42; 43; 150.

S

Salvation or Savior — A major theme running throughout the Bible is that sinful men and women need to be rescued from both the power and the consequences of the sin that they commit. Only one Person has the power and authority to deliver them from their fatal predicament: God. The New Testament explains that God's Son, Jesus Christ, has become the Savior we need through His death and resurrection. All who place their trust in Him will be rescued from the penalty of their sin and receive eternal life.

See Deuteronomy 32:15; 2 Samuel 22:47; 1 Chronicles 16:35; Psalm 42:11; Isaiah 43:11; Luke 2:11; John 4:42; Acts 5:31; 13:23; Philippians 3:20; Titus 1:4; 2:13.

Satan — A spiritual being of great power and evil intelligence who opposes God's work and attacks His people. Apparently he was created as a holy angel but through pride fell from his high place and now leads a doomed rebellion. He has several other names in the Bible, including the "devil," the "serpent," the "dragon," the "evil one" and "Beelzebub."

See 1 Chronicles 21:1; Job 1:6-12; Matthew 4:1-11; John 8:44; Romans 16:20; Ephesians 6:12; Hebrews 2:14-15; 1 Peter 5:8-9; 1 John 3:8; Revelation 20:10.

Second Coming — Hundreds of prophecies pepper the Bible concerning the physical return of Jesus Christ to this earth. Jesus Himself promised many times that, after His resurrection and ascension into heaven, He would one day come back to take all His followers with Him to live with God, both those alive at the time and those who had died.

See Psalm 2:1-12; Daniel 7:13-14; Matthew 24:26-51; Mark 13:26-37; Acts 1:9-11; 1 Thessalonians 4:13—5:11; 2 Thessalonians 2:1-12; Revelation 3:11; 19:11-21.

Sin — Any thought, action, desire, plan, or deed that rejects God's will in favor of an individual's own selfish wishes. A sinful attitude says to God, in words or action, "My will be done" instead of "Your will be done."

See Genesis 39:6-9; Psalm 32:5; 38:18; Ezekiel 18:30-32; Matthew 5:29-30; 18:5-9; Romans 2:12; 14:13; Galatians 3:22; Colossians 3:5-6; Ephesians 5:3-7.

Son of God — See "Jesus Christ."

Soul — An incorporeal and eternal part of every human being, usually associated with the emotions and closely related to the heart. The term can be used to refer to the whole human being, in its totality, or to that part of him or her that is most deeply "him" or "her" and which survives death.

See Deuteronomy 4:29; 6:5; 1 Samuel 1:10; Psalm 6:3; Matthew 10:28; 16:26; 26:38; 1 Thessalonians 5:23; Hebrews 4:12; 1 Peter 2:11.

Spirit — The term can refer to an incorporeal, intelligent being, such as God, angels, or demons; to the disembodied spirit of a human being; to the essence of a human being; or to the dominant disposition of a person ("He has a haughty spirit").

See Job 4:15; 1 Kings 22:21; Psalm 31:5; Proverbs 16:18-19; Isaiah 42:5; Matthew 26:41; Luke 23:46; 24:39; John 4:24; Acts 23:8; Hebrews 12:23; 1 Peter 3:19.

T

Temple — According to the Old Testament, an ornate building was constructed in Jerusalem to house the ark of the covenant–a box covered with gold that contained the ten commandments–the place where God said He would live with His ancient people. In the New Testament, God does not live in a "house of stone," but in the hearts of His people. So the Holy Spirit takes up residence in every believer in Christ.

See 1 Kings 5:3—7:1; 2 Kings 23:26—25:17; Ezra 1:1-4; Zechariah 4:9; Matthew 21:12-15; 24:1-2; John 2:20-21; 1 Corinthians 3:16-17; 6:19; Ephesians 2:21.

Trinity — Although Christians believe in only one God, the Bible also indicates that this solitary God exists in three "Persons": God the Father, God the Son, and God the Holy Spirit. The three Persons, together, make up the single Godhead.

See John 6:27; John 10:30; Romans 8:14; Matthew 28:19-20; Luke 3:21-22; 2 Corinthians 13:14.

Trust — See "faith."

W

Walk with God — The Bible compares a journey of faith with Jesus Christ to a walk with God. Why a walk? Perhaps because a walk has to start someplace; then it goes someplace else, although seldom quickly; it may cover many kinds of terrain (uphill, downhill); it provides plenty of time for conversation; it requires occasional changes of direction; it progresses only through a succession of steps; and it may involve falling and getting back up again.

See Genesis 5:22-24; 17:1; Leviticus 26:12; Deuteronomy 5:33; 10:12; Psalm 128:1; Isaiah 2:5; John 8:12; Romans 4:12; 2 Corinthians 6:16; 1 John 1:6-7; 2:6.

Worship — To enjoy the presence and work of God by honestly and cheerfully expressing back to Him His faithfulness, majesty, greatness, and beauty. Worship may take many forms and may occur in either groups or in solitude, but it always focuses on God Himself.

See Exodus 23:25-26; 34:14; 2 Chronicles 16:29-36; 20:2-28; Psalm 29:2; Matthew 2:2; Luke 4:8; John 4:21-24; Romans 12:1; Hebrews 1:6; 12:28-29.